STIMULATED!

Habits to Spark
Your Creative Genius
at Work

Andrew Pek and Jeannine McGlade

Greenleaf
Book Group LP

Published by Greenleaf Book Group Press
4425 Mo Pac South, Suite 600
Austin, TX 78735

Distributed by Greenleaf Book Group LP

For ordering information or special discounts for bulk purchases, please contact Greenleaf Book Group LP at 4425 Mo Pac South, Suite 600, Longhorn Building, 3rd Floor, Austin, TX 78735, (512) 891-6100.

Design and composition by Greenleaf Book Group LP
Cover design by Greenleaf Book Group LP

Publisher's Cataloging-In-Publication Data
(Prepared by The Donohue Group, Inc.)

Pek, Andrew.
    Stimulated! : habits to spark your creative genius at work / Andrew Pek,
Jeannine McGlade. -- 1st ed.

    p. : ill. ; cm.

    ISBN: 978-1-929774-50-0

1. Creative ability in business. 2. Creative thinking. 3. Success in business.
I. McGlade, Jeannine. II. Title. III. Title: Habits to spark your creative
genius at work

HD53 .P45 2008
650.1   2007941952

Printed in China on acid-free paper

13 12 11 10 09 08   10 9 8 7 6 5 4 3 2 1

First Edition

Acknowledgments

Bernard of Chartres, the 11th century French philosopher, was attributed with saying that "we are like dwarfs on the shoulders of giants, so that we can see more than they, and things at a greater distance, not by virtue of any sharpness of sight on our part, or any physical distinction, but because we are carried high and raised up by their giant size." The clarity of our voice and successful achievement in writing this book would not have been possible had we not been carried high and raised up by the many amazing people who generously shared their experiences and provided us with opportunities in which to observe them, partner with them, and witness how they made the process of being stimulated not a one time act, but a habit. We are deeply thankful to all of them and their many creative actions and results.

Although many of these "stimulated and creative" types appear in this book, there are many other people whose shoulders we stood upon that we wish to thank as well.

Thanks to our publisher Greenleaf Book Group beginning with GBG's creative leaders: Clint Greenleaf and Meg La Borde; Alan Grimes for keeping us on task; Lari Bishop for amplifying our voice through the editing process; Justin Branch for literally opening the doors for us as we made our way into the publishing world; and a special recognition to Lisa Woods, our designer, who was able to pop inside our heads and translate our somewhat 1970s heavy-metal minds into a credible and stimulating form of expression. And to Peg Booth, our publicist, thank you for helping us get our message out to the world.

We would also like to thank all of our associates at növes and the close friends and family who have supported us and our work, helped inspire our own creative genius and took time to give us that all important feedback to improve our book. Thank you Tony Petrella for being there with us right from the start, reminding us to never give up and strive always for richness and reach; John Sganga for your timely business input and suggestions as a trusted advisor and friend; Patti Simigran for sparking our own thinking on what it means to have an edge; Carol Perdic for giving new meaning to the phrase "taste test the product;" Andrea Weiss whose loyalty, friendship, and trust have meant more to us than you'll ever know; and our many other clients who by virtue of their desire to be more innovative and grow gave us the opportunity to spark their creative genius. A special thanks to Pat and Jim McGlade, and Margit Pek, whose inspiring emails, steadfast encouragement, and delicious meals not only kept us well nourished physically and emotionally, but inspired us to keep believing in ourselves because they never stopped believing in us. We love you!

When the concept and spark of this book first burst into our minds we knew we had to walk our talk and find ways to keep ourselves stimulated. Thanks to the individuals featured in this book, having had an opportunity to meet, observe, and partner with so many stimulating people, and having been able to travel to cool spaces and places, the writing of this book was truly fun and we are excited about sharing this with you, the reader, in the hopes that you will find passion, freshness, and be stimulated each and every day.

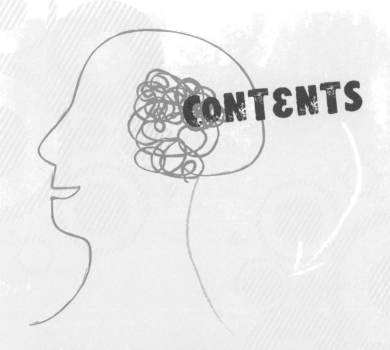

CONTENTS

Awaken Your Creative Genius

A Rainy October Day, Dublin, Ireland

On a rainy October day in Dublin over a cup of hot tea, we were busily preparing for a very exciting and challenging assignment to help an organization double its business in Europe. It was an initiative like no other in the history of the organization. Needless to say, the stakes were high—especially for David, our client.

David had asked to meet with us prior to the kick-off meeting. As we listened to him talk, we were surprised to learn that he was incredibly worried about this project. He felt he had lost his spunk and overall ability to come up with fresh, new ideas. A brand manager by day and a family man by night, he was just plumb exhausted and had seemingly run out of creative juice. He rattled off a list of complaints we had heard many times before from other clients: lack of energy and inspiration, endless amounts of reports, budgets to deal with, spending cutbacks, and general frustration with the bureaucracy he had endured for years. We could sense that it was all finally starting to catch up with him, and he was about to crash.

Looking at David, you'd never know what he was experiencing. On the outside he looked fit and ready to take on the world. We had thought of him as an inspired, engaged, energetic, and passionate professional. As we probed further, we began to see the obvious culprit behind his doubt: a lack of stimulus. He was feeling no excitement, very overwhelmed, a bit bored, discouraged, and unmotivated. Of course, the question then was, how could we help David get stimulated? How could we help him find his energy, his motivation, his excitement? How could we help him get his swing back, ready to tackle the great challenge before him with excitement and passion?

His team and the organization he was working for were not producing many exciting ideas, and the same old actions ruled the day. He admitted that he, too, was out of good stuff and not terribly excited about the prospects of the business plan and the innovation project that lay ahead. When we asked him when he had last come up with a creative idea, he chuckled and said, "I can't remember."

Let's face it, when you are not stimulated it's hard to be excited or look forward to anything. When we don't have much left in our creative tank or we are running on the vapors of ideas gone by, eventually we will simply run out of gas. We imagine that you can relate to David's story. Similar situations arise for so many of us from the craziness of our lives, the unconscious routines we adopt, and the staleness that sets in because of these routines. When we are feeling bored, stale, or stuck, we are likely to be suffering from a lack of stimulus. During these times it's hard to get excited about anything and it's easy to fall into a creative abyss. We become zombies and go through the motions of life, leaving an ever-expanding hole where our creative spark used to be: a "stimulus gap."

This gap is not to be underestimated. It's huge and it's widespread and it's probably affecting the person sitting next to you at this very moment—or worse, you! Filling this gap, and coming back to the land of the living, is what this book is all about. It is a matter of finding, nurturing, and experiencing stimuli of all kinds as part of your daily routine in order to keep things fresh.

You know you're a zombie and need to get out of a stimulus gap if you say yes to any of the following:

* Do you often feel overwhelmed with what you need to do?
* Do you often feel bored?
* Do you have a tendency to "sweat the small stuff" and get caught up in those stressors?
* Do you find it difficult to set aside half an hour a day for yourself?
* Are you feeling "stuck" in life/work?
* Do you feel stuck in a routine?
* Do you feel like you just "don't have the time" to be as creative as you'd like to be?
* Do you find it difficult to take a break and just "do nothing" for a period of time?

HOW DO YOU KNOW IF YOU'RE A

ZOMBIE?

After working for many years in the broad arena of people development, we know one thing for sure. If we become aware of and conscious of how we seek and use stimulus to spark our creative genius, we will flourish; if we don't, well, you know what happens.

STUCK, STALE, AND STRESSED OUT!

Numerous studies show us that stress, if not managed effectively, can lead to burnout. When we are in burnout mode it's hard to access our creativity and even harder to feel passion and excitement about the challenges and opportunities we face each and every day. The way we see it, burnout and the lack of creative energy go hand in hand. If you are feeling stress and don't know quite how to manage it, there are many resources available, including good books such as *The Stress of Life,* by Hans Selye, and *StressMap: Personal Diary Edition,* developed by Essi Systems. In the meantime, to minimize stress and maximize your creative energy, try the following tips.

Change Your Routine Even small changes to your everyday routine will give you a burst of freshness and perhaps new perspective and resolve to take on the challenges ahead.

Change the Way You Think The brain is a very powerful tool. We are motivated by our current dominant thought. If you are thinking of negative things or find yourself indulging in negative self-talk ("I'm not good at this," or "I can't get this done"), change your thinking to something positive or inspiring. At a minimum, engage yourself in positive self-talk to break the cycle of negative thoughts. This will help get your creative juices flowing!

Visualize Success In a moment of stress or a lull in your creative energy, visualize a successful outcome. Ask yourself, What's my goal? and make it your dominant thought as you take one small step at a time to move in the direction of the goal.

See RED (Rest, Exercise, and Diet) We all know that getting plenty of rest, exercising, and eating a healthy, well-balanced diet helps to decrease the negative effects of stress. Here are some things that help us see RED: a nap during the day (yes, even at work!), a walk at lunch, and a handful of delicious walnuts (or our favorite, tamari-spiced almonds) from a local health food store.

Laugh Trying to find the humor in all situations (or memories of a humorous situation) will break the cycle of stress and diminish the tension you feel in the moment. Tell yourself a good joke, call up a friend who makes you laugh, or go people watching—this always brings a smile to our faces!

Evolution, Creation, and Stimulation

If feeling more alive and excited about work and life isn't enough to inspire you, perhaps you should think about evolution—that's right, evolution. Each of us has an evolutionary need to create. From the first language systems and the first wheel to the airplane and our many forms of modern technology, the new ideas and developments of each age have borne witness to humanity's insatiable drive to adapt what we have in front of us. That drive is crucial to our success. It's not the strongest who survive, but the ones who adapt best. And in order to adapt, we need to create, and in order to create, we need stimulus, and in order to get stimulus, well, you need to read this book! Seriously, the need to create is a basic human need that, it could be argued, is not only an evolutionary imperative, but a spiritual one as well.

BLOCKED CREATIVE EXPRESSION IS AS DETRIMENTAL TO YOUR WELL-BEING AS A DRUG ADDICTION.

—CAROLINE MYSS, AUTHOR OF
Invisible Acts of Power

According to Caroline Myss, author of *Invisible Acts of Power: Channeling Grace in Your Everyday Life*, "Every single person is born with something to create—that creation might be a child or a business or a garden or a circle of friends or a peace accord. Whatever it is will be personally beneficial as well as beneficial for others." Myss reports that when people aren't doing what they are called to do or when they feel stuck or uninspired—in our parlance, not stimulated—she sees ill heath, stress, and chronic suffering time and time again.

> Creativity is often misapprehended as a purely artistic or intellectual inclination . . . but working with your creative energy is as essential to your health and overall well-being as breathing and eating. Creative energy is a basic survival instinct; it motivates us to become part of society, to become productive, bring things to life, and to distinguish ourselves from others by what we make, the crafts we pursue, the skills we develop in business or in cultivating friendships, the entrepreneurial

ideas we conceive, the problems we resolve, and the children or communities we birth and nurture. Yet many people have creative ideas and yearnings that they do not pursue out of a fear of financial failure or embarrassment, or because they are reluctant to step outside of their normal way of life and change it.

Myss makes the point that whatever the creation, it is critical that we each create. Imagine a world without creative expression—no artistic masterpieces, no music on the go, no overnight mail, no instant communication with your family in the next room or a stranger across the globe. Creativity is vital to advancing society and our potential as individuals. Each of us has the ability to leave a unique thumbprint on our world, and we do so through our creative expression. As you read, interact with, and put into practice the stories, exercises, and tools in this book, think about your circumstances at work and at home so that you can find the answers that will help motivate and inspire you and give you the creative energy necessary to live a meaningful and rich life.

Once you realize you are already creative (and you *are* already creative!), find new ways of creating the right conditions to get stimulated, and understand that getting stimulated and being creative are a way of life, then you will be on an exciting lifelong journey that will leave you and those around you inspired.

The many people and organizations we have had the privilege to work with, learn from, and "study" have produced creative expressions ranging from converting mouthwash into "film strips" and implementing widespread organizational change to launching on-demand TV platforms and inventing a natural remedy to heal wounds. While what they actually did was different, each demonstrated a pattern of behavior that could be considered magical, a gift of creativity bestowed only upon them. However, the individuals and teams who came up with these wonderful innovations were not necessarily creative in the way many of us imagine when we think of creative individuals.

Typically, when people think about someone creative, they tend to head straight toward the Picassos of the world. Of course Picasso was an extraordinary creative talent. However, it's not about being Picasso—there are many hardworking "regular" men and women who have produced many creative outcomes over their lifetimes. How'd they do it? Well, they become like Picasso, perhaps, and, by implementing a specific set of habits on a daily basis, they maintain a regular state of stimulation. Without these habits they couldn't get stimulated, and without getting stimulated, they couldn't be creative, and without being creative, they couldn't be innovative. Cultivating these habits (which you will learn about shortly) will give you the potential to become extraordinarily creative.

INSPIRATION DOES EXIST BUT IT MUST FIND YOU WORKING.

—Pablo Picasso, Spanish Cubist painter

THE EXTRAORDINARILY ORDINARY CREATIVE

You don't need the next Picasso to teach you to be creative. In fact, often it is the more ordinary creatives we can learn the most from, and whose example we can use for sparking our own creative genius. So, as you are thinking about becoming more Picasso-like, take some time to answer the following questions:

Think of someone who you think is creative.

- Why do you feel she is creative?
- What specifically does she do that makes her creative?

Now, think of your own creative expression and ideas.

- What can you learn about creativity from this person?
- What can you take from how this person behaves and apply to your own creative expression?
- How might you implement one of these behaviors tomorrow as you go about stimulating your creative genius?

Whatever your incentive to be creative, the question now is, How can I become and stay creatively fit to adapt to the ever-changing world and stay effectively engaged, stimulated, and motivated to create that which will do great things for me, my team, my family, and my organization? For starters, we need a plan, a regimen, a road map, a framework for getting stimulated—a way to ready ourselves to create.

INVIGORATE

FUN

ACTION

EXCITEMENT

ROUSE TO ACTION

ALIVE

PASSION

CREATIVE

SPARK

IGNITE

MOTIVATED

ENERGY

POSSIBILITIES

IMAGINATION

The key question isn't "What fosters creativity?" But it is why in God's name isn't everyone creative? Where was the human potential lost? How was it crippled? I think therefore a good question might be not why do people create? But why do people not create or innovate? We have got to abandon that sense of amazement in the face of creativity, as if it were a miracle if anybody created anything.

—ABRAHAM MASLOW, AMERICAN PSYCHOLOGIST

Stimulus: The Catalyst that Sparks Your Creative Genius

What do you think of when you see the word *stimulus*? We're sure all sorts of images come to mind (some that make you smile, laugh, or maybe even blush!). We've shared some of our associations on the opposite page—feel free to add your own!

We don't know about you, but these words bring us energy! We feel stimulated just talking about stimulus! But where does this whole idea of stimulus fit into the larger picture of creativity and innovation?

We see stimulus as the pre-state, if you will, to creativity. In other words, in order for you to create or get creative ideas, something needs to happen *beforehand* to jump-start your creative action. That something is the stimulus. For most, stimulus is often completely random and unexpected—we don't know how or why the lightbulb goes on, but it does. For example, have you ever been singing your favorite tune while driving, walking, or taking a shower and suddenly the creative juices start to flow and ideas and thoughts pop into your mind? Have you ever stopped to think about what it was that set these good feelings and ideas in motion? If you're like most people, you don't necessarily stop and think about what got you to that moment—you're just glad you got there at all! Most of us don't question it. More often we can only tell you why when we are feeling less than creative or when we are stuck—just as David was on that fateful morning in Dublin.

INNOVATION
IS NOT A BIG LIGHTBULB,
BUT MANY POINTS OF LIGHT THAT
HELP TO ILLUMINATE
THE POSSIBILITIES.

—Dave Raath, head of innovation
and product development,
Johnson and Johnson, South Africa

For us, being stimulated is about expressing, practicing, and developing the habits of creative thinking and action. This book reminds us to explore ourselves and our environment, and to bring creative energy into our work, meetings, and interactions with others every day, as a way of life. Being stimulated requires that we work more with imagination than knowledge, celebrate failures as well as successes, reward risk, and pursue ideas that others might think crazy.

The Habits that Spark Your Creative Genius

In the many years we have helped organizations effect change, build leaders, develop high-performing teams, and grow the business and the employees within, we have consistently observed a set of specific behaviors (habits) that, working in harmony with one another, help people to be stimulated and ultimately spark creative genius.

We believe that every human being has the potential to cultivate and demonstrate these habits and in so doing, will unleash his creative genius. Human minds, bodies, and souls are equipped with a highly creative ability to sense things and also act on them in ingenious and industrious ways. While we constantly interact with our environment, our creative genius lingers in the background, waiting to be activated to produce creative expressions (style) and impressions (impact). For example, when a musician plays music, how he performs that music (tempo, tone, melody, style, and selection) is his expression, while the music he produces is the impression (the feeling and emotion) he leaves with others. The beauty of creative genius is that we have many creative expressions to choose from and consequently we can form many different impressions. Our creative expressions and impressions are the result of using these habits that we consciously nurture. By nurturing them, we nourish our appetite for creating and stimulating the creative potential in others.

The more that we stimulate our creativity the greater the likelihood we will produce creative expressions and impressions that yield advancement opportunities. It is cyclical and it builds momentum as our creative output increases. By developing our creative expressions and impressions through various sensing and action-oriented habits, we will naturally attract "sparks of creativity" or help advance creative insights on a more regular and high-quality basis.

We have identified five specific habits that work in harmony with one another to shape the anatomy of creative genius:

- **Scouting** forms the backbone of our creative anatomy. Scouting contains the essential orientation and energy we need to find, observe, and use to interact with stimulus and initiate the creative cycle we each possess.

- **Cultivating** is the habit of creating, growing, and developing the spaces and places in which sparks become possible and you are in a creative state of mind. Without fertile conditions, a proper environment in which to be inspired, your creative genius will not flourish and attracting sparks will be more difficult.

- **Playing** represents a childlike state that helps us to feel at ease in "experimenting" with stimulus and maintaining a perpetual state of curiosity in pursuit of creative insight and spark moments.

- **Venturing** is the essential habit of encouraging our hearts as well as our minds to make a leap into sometimes unknown—and often a bit scary—territory. It is through venturing that we develop nerve and decide to either pursue a spark of inspiration or not.

- **Harvesting** is turning our sparks and ideas into something that is real and of value to ourselves and to others. Harvesting is where we yield and celebrate real results—those things that you can see, touch, feel, and experience that manifest as a result of all the hard work and energy of sparking your creative genius.

This book grows directly from our experiences and conversations with thousands of people we have encountered on our journey thus far. It aims to help everyone be more creative and get more stimulated in work, in relationships, and in life. This book is also a reflection of our experiences trying to stimulate our own individual creative genius. What we've learned is that not only do the encounters of other people confirm our position, but they also provide rich insights on effective ways to spark your own creative genius, to crawl out of a slump when the juices don't seem to be flowing, and to solve important, pressing challenges with a new, fresh approach.

Our goal in this book is for you to learn from our experiences, as well as from the experiences of some of the people we met, how the habits we put forth work and how being stimulated is a significant factor in inspiring and sustaining your creative side more consistently. We hope that as a result of reading and interacting with this book you will have more moments when the creative action flows. More importantly, we hope you will know how to go after the stimulus necessary to get you to that point. This book puts you in touch with your sources of creativity and helps you increase your hunger for gathering insights, generating ideas, and driving creative solutions that help you both personally and professionally. The results of these habits and sustained efforts will not only give you the extra energy and creativity you crave, but they will also have enormous impact on the people you interact with, the organizations that you are a part of,

The Habits that Spark
Your Creative Genius:

SCOUTING
CULTIVATING
PLAYING
VENTURING
HARVESTING

and the teams you lead or participate in—where people are counting on you to perform as your complete, creative self. The additional benefit—one that we believe is critical for living a fulfilling life and ultimately reinforces more creativity—is a feeling of joy, passion, and energy.

Simple, practical, and fun, this book is full of stories about individuals who pursue their own creative impulses and are rewarded by the satisfaction of breakthrough results. We've introduced the specific habits that will help you embark on an exciting journey of personal discovery, creative confidence, and increased energy. In short, we want to help you get and remain stimulated. We hope that as you begin to nurture these habits you will find yourself feeling more alive and excited about your work and your life because you are inspired more often.

You may be wondering whatever happened to stressed-out, overwhelmed, understimulated David from Dublin. Well, the good news is that he ultimately went on to lead his team to great success, and after getting the team heading in a positive direction, he realized he needed more stimulus and passion in both his personal and professional lives. He picked up and dusted off his old electric guitar and started taking lessons again, which gave him a creative outlet from which to draw even more inspiration. He eventually accepted a new position in a smaller organization that gives him more opportunity to utilize his creative talents. When we asked him about the difficult time he had at his former job, he answered, "It didn't kill me, so I guess it made me stronger. Once I knew what was missing and I got out and got more stimulated, I was able to see more clearly what I needed to do—both personally and professionally. Being conscious of the moments when I felt a spark—and the moments when I didn't—started to give me the clues I needed to help uncover the mystery of why I was feeling the way I was feeling. It was a big help to just be conscious and focus on de-stressing my life. Once I did that, I was able to open up the creative outlet and things started to flow."

He told us that once he realized what he was missing, he took every opportunity to get out and about and stimulate his senses to give him new perspective and freshness. He is sure that this is what helped him come up with new ideas during the project as well as figure out what he needed to do to bring the passion and excitement back into his life.

How do we learn from a story like David's while honoring our own unique situations, preferences, and constraints to awaken our creative genius? To start, we need know-how about stimulus combined with action and a commitment to develop and implement new habits that will lead us to our creative genius. If you're ready to discover with us, play with us, and learn with us, let's get busy and explore more closely the path that will lead you to your creative genius!

CHAPTER 2

Stimulus: The Catalyst for Creative Genius

One morning in 1971, Bill Bowerman sat down to breakfast with his wife and was immediately entranced by the plate of waffles in front of him. In that moment, through a spark of inspiration, he clearly saw the future of running shoes and training techniques—two things he had obsessed about all his life.

Soon after that morning, Bowerman began pouring rubber into his wife's waffle iron. From his experiments in his kitchen, he created a revolutionary running-shoe sole that gave birth to the business juggernaut that keeps creating and innovating. That business is called Nike.

Bowerman's moment of inspiration was no accident. Like so many creative-innovator types, Bowerman was often deeply immersed in trying to solve a problem or look for a better way. Running was always his muse. He was a very successful track and field coach, having trained thirty-one Olympic athletes, fifty-one all-Americans, twelve American record-holders, twenty-four NCAA champions, and sixteen sub-four-minute-milers. His dedication to helping runners ran so deep that he and his partner Phil Knight felt that "anyone with a body" could be an athlete who could have fun through fitness. Because of Bowerman's unyielding passion for running and his commitment to advancing the performance of athletes and athletic products, he had many spark moments throughout his career; he could not *not* be attracted to sparks that kept him focused on his goal, his passion.

The Spark Moment

If you have ever fallen in love, you know life can feel wonderful. Other than the person you are in love with, nothing else in life seems to matter—you go without food, you go without sleep, and you spend all of your idle time daydreaming about the other person. These tingly sensations and sleepless nights may also arise when you have a creative spark. Like magic, an unexplained sensation of joy can occur at any time and may surge so strongly through your mind and body that you say to yourself, "Eureka! I have an idea! And I love it!"

When we engage with stimulus in a habitual and conscious way, we open ourselves to being struck by a sensation many refer to as an aha! moment. We refer to these moments as spark moments, instances when you take notice of a particular stimulus and the sensation and thought it provokes in you. Spark moments seemingly come out of nowhere and trigger the creation of an idea. Like the lover whose eyes you cannot look away from, a stimulus has grabbed all of your attention. This spark moment activates a signal—an electrical charge if you will—telling you to take note.

When we routinely put ourselves into situations where spark moments can occur, we set off a wonderful chain of events that may ultimately lead to big, bold ideas. Stimulus is the necessary catalyst to attract spark moments on a regular basis. Spark moments are the precursors to having great ideas, unlocking your creative genius, and inspiring creative action. Not only is this whole process fun, but there's science behind why spark moments are so powerful and so necessary to the creative process.

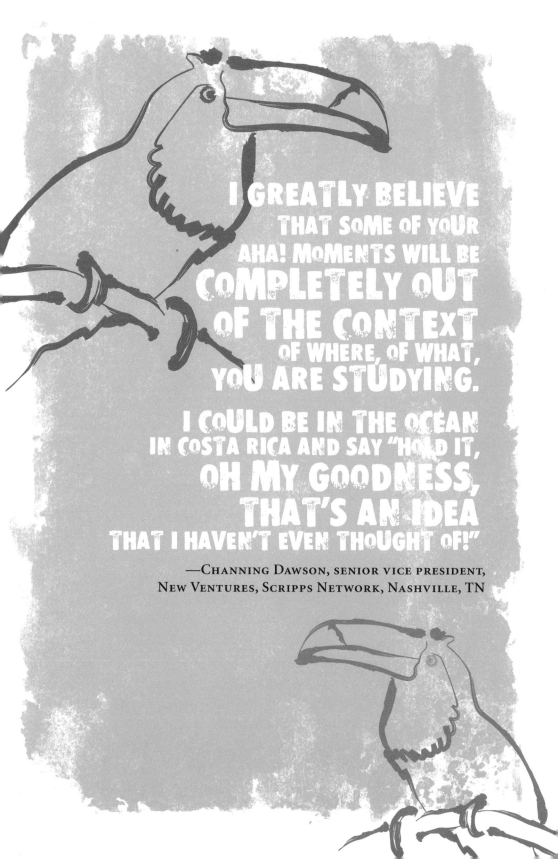

I GREATLY BELIEVE THAT SOME OF YOUR AHA! MOMENTS WILL BE COMPLETELY OUT OF THE CONTEXT OF WHERE, OF WHAT, YOU ARE STUDYING.

I COULD BE IN THE OCEAN IN COSTA RICA AND SAY "HOLD IT, OH MY GOODNESS, THAT'S AN IDEA THAT I HAVEN'T EVEN THOUGHT OF!"

—Channing Dawson, senior vice president, New Ventures, Scripps Network, Nashville, TN

CREATIVITY AND CREATIVE EXPRESSION = STIMULUS + INTENSITY + WHERE, WHAT, WHO + VARIETY + FREQUENCY

The Science Behind the Spark Moment

In any good science experiment, you need a stimulus, and you need to monitor the effect of that stimulus on the environment or the object you are testing. In the case of creativity and coming up with ideas, the spark moment is what begins a chain reaction of converting an aha! or hunch into an insight or idea. Of course, a spark won't lead to a creative impulse in all cases. When a spark moment occurs, a combination of conscious reflection and action is necessary to advance that moment into a creative idea or expression. The impulses of creativity and creative expression are sustained based on the intensity of stimulus; where, what, or who that stimulus comes from; the variety of the stimulus; and the frequency.

Although it is sometimes difficult to grasp (or be aware of) the full nature of a spark moment and its impact on our creative state of being, intentional exposure and interaction with stimuli that enable spark moments is unmistakably a key dynamic to cultivating and unleashing our creative genius. Let's try an exercise that reveals some basic information about how we process stimuli.

Say the following *colors* aloud—not the word, but the color of each word. See how fast you can do it with no errors.

BLUE	RED	YELLOW
BROWN	ORANGE	BLACK
PURPLE	GOLD	WHITE
PINK	SILVER	GREEN

So, what happened? How'd you do? Were you able to flawlessly read the *colors* versus the words? It's easy to mess this up, at least until you get into a rhythm. We tend to read the *words* more easily than the colors, at least initially. This is known as the Stroop Effect, named after the man who identified this interesting phenomenon, J. Ridley Stroop. Researchers attribute this effect to what they refer to as selective attention and speed of processing. Essentially, we can read words more quickly than we can name the colors, and naming the color of a written word (especially a word that is a color) requires more attention and thoughtfulness than reading a word. Our sense of sight interprets these words quickly and immediately sends that interpretation to our brains, where we make sense of the stimulus. Because the directions to this game are to read the colors, not the words themselves, our brains receive the stimulus (the word) and are immediately presented with a problem that needs to be solved. The stimulus received needs to be reinterpreted to play the game.

Becoming more aware of how your senses capture different stimuli can help you tune in to and receive varied stimuli that will help lead to inspired action or creativity. Let's talk about the importance of our five wonderful senses: touch, taste, smell, hearing, and sight.

Coming to Your Senses: The Brain and Stimulus

Our senses are the physical means by which we take in information and send it to our brains for processing. Without our senses, not only would life be pretty bland, but we would have a hard time gathering information about our world. Our brains are lush mechanisms that, upon receiving some sort of stimulus, create images and associations that help us go about the business of our lives, interpret information, recall memories, and create new ideas. For example, have you ever smelled something or heard a song that brought back specific memories from your childhood? Or have you seen a road sign or heard a DJ talking on the radio while you are driving to work and remembered something you need to do? These stimuli are captured by our brains and trigger ideas, thoughts, or memories.

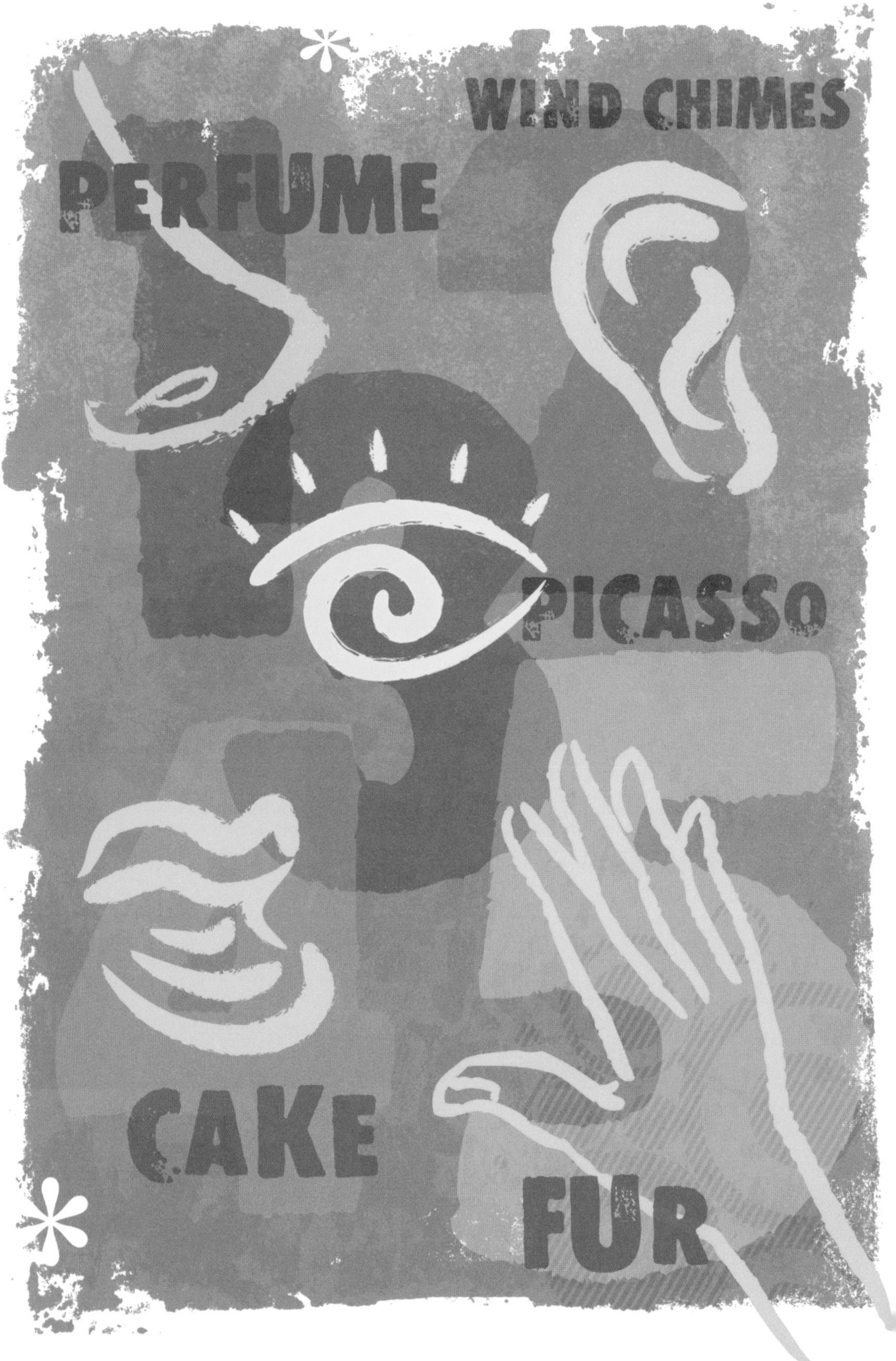
WIND CHIMES
PERFUME
PICASSO
CAKE
FUR

DID YoU KNoW . . .?

Did you know that a dog has 200 million smell cells in its nose—forty times as many as our human noses?

Did you know that your eye color is dictated by where your ancestors lived? According to Roizen and Oz, typically people from sunny environments had dark irises in order to block out the sun, whereas people who lived in darker environments with less ambient light had blue eyes so that their eyes could let in more light.

Our sense organs (nose, eyes, ears, tongue, and skin) start to work when something "stimulates special nerve cells called receptors . . . Once stimulated, the receptors send nerve impulses along sensory nerves to the brain. Your brain tells you what the stimulus is" (www.thinkquest.org). And, of course, once your brain tells you what the stimulus is, it starts to make sense out of the stimulus—making associations, thinking about implications, giving meaning, and creating abundant possibilities. As Kenneth A. Wesson suggests, it is when we put ourselves in a position to have many sensory experiences that possibilities become limitless. As we stimulate our brains and expose ourselves to varied stimuli, we are more likely to have spark moments that ultimately lead to new insights, ideas, and innovations. According to Wesson:

> Greater brain stimulation promotes an increase in the number of dendrites ("little trees") connecting the billions of cells in the brain. Neurons sprout and re-sprout new dendrites, connecting more and more brain cells throughout one's life, giving all of us the neurophysiologic wherewithal to learn throughout our entire lifetime.
>
> Multi-sensory experiences further extend these plentiful and precious connections throughout the entire cerebral cortex and they form additional links with other sub-cortical structures inside the brain. Conversely, reducing the quantity and/or quality of experiences and learning opportunities diminishes the brain's neural pathways, permanently

decreasing one's ability to learn. However, the human brain is capable of creating trillions of interrelated neural networks rendering our capacity to learn virtually limitless.

So, if you are asking yourself, "All this is very interesting, but so what?" here's the so what: by allowing ourselves more opportunities to get stimulated through varied sensory experiences we open ourselves up to a world of limitless possibilities to create! Each and every one of us has the ability to create because each and every one of us uses our five senses. The more we use them, the more possibilities we'll have.

TO BE CREATIVE, YOU GOTTA LOVE TO TOUCH, FEEL, AND TASTE.

—Shelley Walsh, VP of design
and visual merchandising,
Tabi International, Canada

Now let's assume that you do have a spark moment. That moment in and of itself isn't the end of the creative process. Of course, coming up with insights or ideas might feel good, but truly advancing your creative genius requires that you take action—creative action. Without creative action we only go so far and do not maximize the potential of our creative genius. Understanding how we consciously attain, interact with, and develop habits to convert spark moments into breakthrough ideas is what makes "stimulus" and being "stimulated" the cornerstone of unlocking your creative genius.

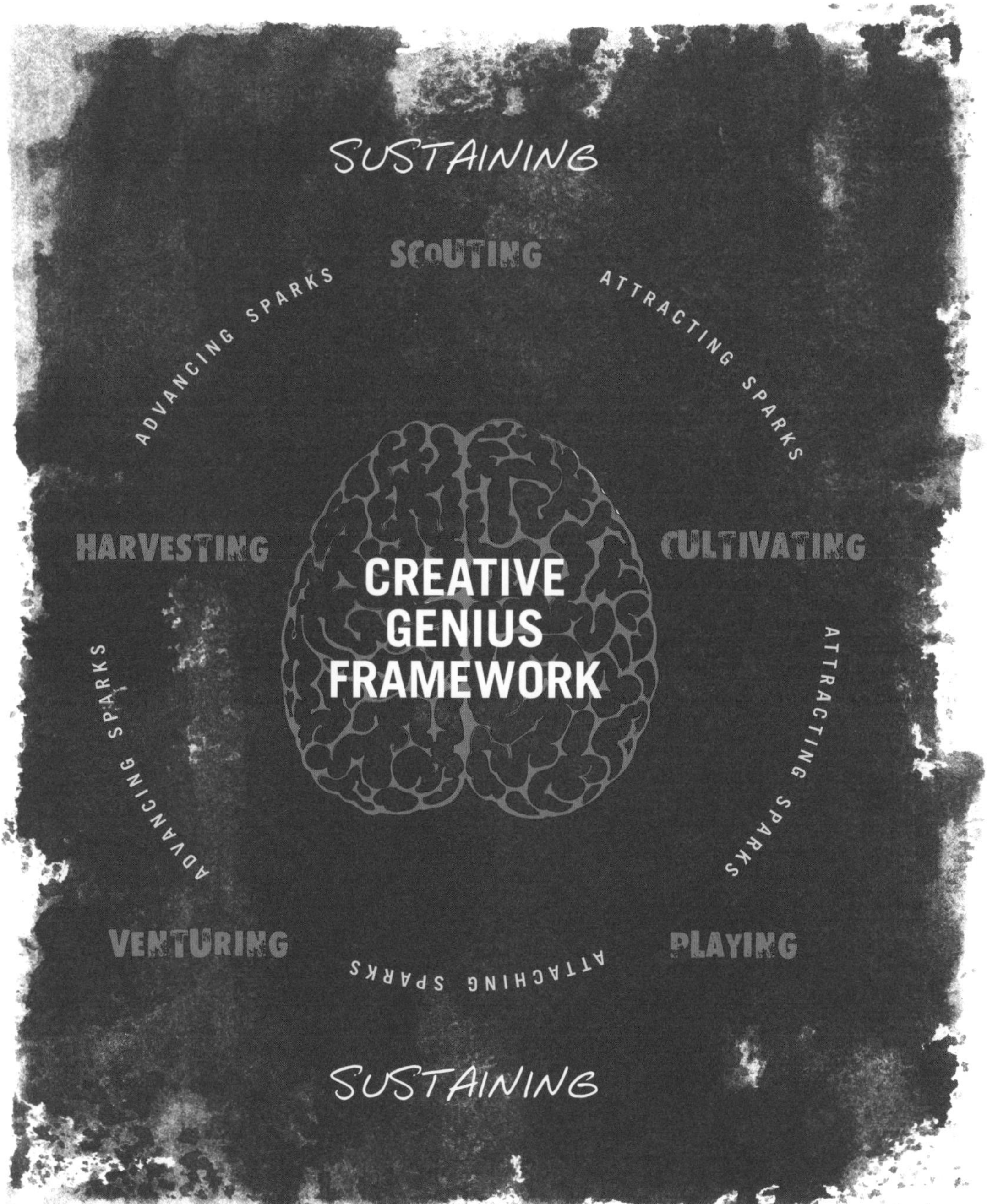

The Cycle of Creative Genius

The following diagram depicts a framework for how you might under-stand and develop the habits for sparking your creative genius. What's important to remember is that although we outline this cycle step-by-step, accessing your creative genius is not a linear process; it is cyclical and doesn't follow a discrete pattern each and every time. However, there are clear habits that we can develop in order to encourage sparks to occur and to fully experience our creative genius.

Attracting spark moments typically begins with scouting. Scouting gets you in touch with the world and puts you in a position to have spark moments because you go out and about with "new" eyes—looking at things differently, taking it all in without evaluating.

As we scout, we also need to cultivate our environment—the spaces and places where we seek, spark, and sustain our creative processes.

While we take in the world and fertilize the soil where ideas can grow, it's important to also remember to play. To play is to experiment, have fun, and let loose in ways that help you to feel more at ease and open to possibility.

These three habits (scouting, cultivating, and playing) are all about attracting spark moments into our purview. At some point, we attach to these sparks and consciously decide whether or not we want to advance them into tangible ideas.

To enable tangible results, the habits of venturing and harvesting are necessary. We venture—take a leap—into unknown territory in order to advance our sparks. Venturing is all about being brave, taking chances, and taking a plunge into potentially uncertain areas of opportunity that at first may feel foreign and uncomfortable. Then we harvest the results of our hard work and ideas. We view harvesting as not only the consequence of your creative efforts, but also as a ritualistic and celebratory effort at sustaining your creative genius. The more creative outcomes we reap as by-products of exercising our creative genius, the more motivated we are to stimulate and produce additional creative results. Harvesting, like the other habits, becomes contagious when we exercise it on a regular basis.

While each habit is different, they are interrelated. We recommend that you apply and sustain each of these habits simultaneously to keep you in a regular state of stimulation. The more you develop each habit in connection with the others, the more your creative genius will grow and consequently produce stimulating outcomes.

Spark at First Sight—Attracting Stimulus

Like when we are falling in love, when we are seeking to be more creative and generate creative solutions to change, we often find ourselves attracted to moments that all of a sudden spark our imagination. The lightbulb goes on and we begin to ponder the implications—sometimes rapidly, sometimes methodically. Our heart starts to race toward a destination and usually unknown path that signals excitement. The adrenalin from the spark of a good idea starts our creative juices flowing. This is what we call the "spark attraction phase," the moment when an idea, thought, or aha! has us lovestruck and our minds, hearts, and even our bodies feel that tingly sensation that says we are on to something—we're stimulated and we crave more.

LOVE AT FIRST SIGHT

Many researchers are now claiming that falling in love, the process of attraction, doesn't happen over time, but instead within minutes—that's right, minutes! (That explains the whole speed-dating phenomenon!) According to an article published in the *Journal of Social and Personal Relationships*, researchers showed that the first few minutes of meeting someone have "a huge influence on the course the relationship will ultimately take." So, your mother was right, first impressions do count!

When creative people start popping with ideas, it's likely that a stimulus of some kind has sparked a sensation, a glimmer of an idea that they can't help but start running with. When this happens, we may lose our appetite, need less sleep, and prefer to spend hours at a time daydreaming about the spark that has struck us so profoundly. In our first book, *növes: recipes for growth and innovation*, we talked about Dan Cudzik of Reynolds Metals, the fellow who invented the stay-on tab, and how he spent many sleepless nights in passionate pursuit of something that would prevent the needless littering of ring tabs and seal cans of soda. Through one spark after the other, Cudzik passionately pursued many different avenues to stimulate ideas, such as visiting stores, reading magazines, using plywood to prototype solutions, and initiating conversations to validate hunches. Finding the stimulus that creates the spark moment—the thing that attracts you to an idea possibility—is key to igniting your creative genius.

Based on our research and our own experiences, we *can* create more of these spark moments and improve our attraction ratio of ideas by routinely putting ourselves in situations where there are opportunities for those moments to occur. Think of it as a kind of dating and mating process. The more we make ourselves "available," the more we begin to signal the message "Take a chance on me!"

YOUR IMAGINATION CREATES THE INNER PICTURE THAT ALLOWS YOU TO PARTICIPATE IN THE ACT OF CREATION.

—DR. WAYNE DYER,
AUTHOR OF *The Power of Intention*

We believe that as you open yourself up more and more to the possibilities, the laws of attraction start to have influence on your actions and spark moments occur with increasing regularity. It's a cyclical process; the more we put ourselves into these situations, the more opportunities to have spark moments and the more opportunity for creative ideas. And the more creative ideas you have, the more energy you will have to encourage new ideas and continue to learn and accomplish more. Once attracted to some inkling of an idea, we want to explore it further and start to from a mental picture of implementing or making the idea real.

At the time a spark occurs it has just enough impact to stimulate your interest and attention. At some point, however, this sensation will go away, evolve into something else, or begin to bring up further interest with questions such as "Hey, what's really going on here?" "Is this something I should stick with or not?" "Is there something to this spark—perhaps the glimmer of an idea?" It is at this precise moment, sometimes consciously and sometimes unconsciously, that you reach a decision point and more seriously evaluate the spark that caught your attention. If you are with others when this spark occurs, it can be helpful to discuss your questions to validate the spark and its "value." Whether or not this is the next breakthrough idea for your organization or the next step in your personal journey, the fact that it has grabbed your attention at all brings you to a decision point. Will I step in further? Is this worth exploring more? Do I give this spark more energy and attention to see where it leads me? The decision is yours: get attached or move on?

Going with It: Attaching to the Spark

When you reach that decisive moment, you are picking up on a different sort of spark—a spark that may in some cases send you very different and conflicting signals. From the moment you first experienced the impulse to the point when you start stepping back, you are consciously or unconsciously deciding whether or not you should pursue a more serious relationship with this spark of an idea. This new sensation of questioning and validating and longing all at the same time signals the stage we refer to as the attachment stage. Attachment is a more contemplative stage than

WHEN YOU ARE **INSPIRED,**
DORMANT FORCES,
FACULTIES, AND TALENTS
BECOME ALIVE.

—PATANJALI, INDIAN COMPILER OF THE YOGA SUTRA

attraction, in which a more analytical mind-set and set of skills start to kick in. It is a deeper, sometimes longer-lasting commitment to the spark of an idea, the critical point where you decide whether or not you will invest in nurturing the spark, or "go steady," so to speak.

You know you are starting to become attached when you notice an ever-increasing devotion to the forming idea, but you still may not be quite sure if it is something you want to act on. On one hand, you may be absolutely smitten with your spark to the point that you reject any variations or new information. Or, as you get closer to the spark, you may feel a bit nervous and express reservations about whether to commit. Either way, you might feel a certain amount of vulnerability and awareness of risk starting to seep into your psyche. This is a natural part of the attachment phase. The viability of any idea worth pursuing has been questioned at some point or another. We put every decision we make, whether business or personal, through a questioning and consideration period. We refer to this as whole brain thinking. It's not just about the creative spark (usually a right-brained function); it's also about a more linear, converging, and analytical approach (characteristic of the left side of the brain) that helps us determine the viability of the spark and whether or not the spark is worth attaching to.

While working with Rick Dzavik, the former European head of innovation at a large consumer health-care organization, we asked him about his experiences with stimulus and the experience of having to commit to certain ideas when they popped. With a smile, he replied,

> We had many moments along our innovation journey where we were not certain if the process of change in our culture would get any legs. It seemed like every other day we would fall in and out of love with our ideas, actions, and programs related to innovation. For years we even struggled to define what we meant by innovation. During the phase in which we launched many innovation initiatives we had many battles. There were many who were not as interested or stimulated about our approaches and it did influence our confidence in our ideas. But about eighteen months into our effort, beyond the initial honeymoon phase,

things started to click and it was at this point many colleagues began to glom on to the process.

Creative sparks work that way. For what may seem like a long period of time we may be infatuated with an idea or set of ideas and processes before we venture into a deeper form of commitment. "Having had a single voice in the beginning—someone who was willing to take some risks, was key to gaining traction and getting others to commit," says Dzavik.

COMMITMENT QUESTIONS

These questions will give you a sense of whether or not your spark is worth committing to:

- Is this spark (or idea) something that is a top priority for you?
- How much risk are you willing to take in order to pursue this further?
- How much time are you willing to invest in this spark (or idea)?
- What is the impact of acting on this spark for yourself? Others?
- What is the cost of not acting? What will you miss? How might you feel if you didn't move forward?
- What support or resources will you need to pursue this spark?
- Does this spark (idea) meet your goals—either personally or professionally?

If the relationship between you and an idea is going to last, you have to form more of an attachment to it and, as Dzavik suggests, have a say in it. However, having a voice and making a sort of public vow to associate ourselves with a given idea involves risk. To create and be creative takes courage, and it takes time to feel secure in fastening ourselves toward any one idea or another. Just because we are enthused about the aha! does not necessarily mean we will stay connected to it. However, when we do, then we are ready to advance our creative efforts to bring about success, much the way Bill Bowerman achieved it in a revolutionary running shoe, or

Dan Cudzik in the stay-on tab, or the many others whose stories we will share with you throughout this book.

Advancing the Spark: Steps Toward Creative Action

Even in the best of circumstances, ambiguity is a part of the creative sparking process. While we may be swept up in the attraction of a new idea or a new trend, let's face it, when it comes time to really commit, many of us get cold feet. How many times have you had a spark moment, come up with a brilliant idea, didn't bother pursuing it, and, just when you weren't looking, someone else put the idea into action? If this has ever happened to you, you know how upsetting it can be. It's hard work to advance our creative genius and the many potentially great ideas we have percolating and steeping in our minds. It takes a lot of energy not only to bring forth ideas, but to maintain them and evolve them to the point where they can become the next big innovation.

However, like anything we do, when it comes to producing results, if we do not add fuel to the fire, then the spark, the flame, will go out. That single committed voice that Dzavik spoke about could just as easily become a faint sound in the wilderness—especially if it is without other voices to support it. It takes a village of individuals to share in the creation process and help nurture and grow ideas—it's tough to go it alone. So, whether the ideas percolating in your mind are ones to grow your business or ones to grow yourself as you journey through this world, having a support system to help you keep them percolating goes a long way.

Creative individuals, people who make it a habit to engage stimulus and generate sparks to awaken their creative mind, make it clear that even with a support group, expressing yourself involves risk. But the rewards can be great once you have finally found something, some idea or notion or plan that you feel will have significant impact and that you are emotionally bound and determined to make real.

Twyla Tharp is one of America's greatest choreographers. She began her career in 1965 and has created more than 130 dances for her company. In her book, *The Creative Habit—Learn It and Use It for Life*, Tharp speaks about the importance of commitment from others. She writes,

> With my dancers, for example, I have an annoying need for proof of their allegiance to me and my projects. So I'm always running through a mental checklist to see if their work habits are as exacting as mine, searching with forensic intensity for evidence of their commitment. Do they show up on time for rehearsal? Are they warmed up? Does their energy flag when rehearsals break down or are they committed to pushing forward?

During the stage of attraction we are pushing ourselves forward but we may also, as Tharp suggests (especially in the early stages of attracting sparks), need the support and commitment of others to propel ideas forward. Seldom does a creative spark advance into something of value without the help of others. Creative ideas flourish best when others become committed.

There comes a time along the creative genius's journey, however, when we involve ourselves completely and vow to stick with the development of an idea until it has taken flight. Once we have decided to leap forward, we are at the stage of the process we call advancement. This advancement is what propels creative action to take place—we are now on to doing what needs to be done to make these ideas/sparks real.

Once you dedicate yourself to your sparks, you can accomplish great things. Benjamin Franklin, for example, was committed to individual and civic advancement. He made his mark on U.S. history and the world with his many remarkable inventions, including bifocals, street lighting, and street cleaning, not to mention his principal role in advancing the development of the United States. Going from a childhood of poverty to a successful career as a merchant and a role as a leader of the American Revolution, Franklin exhibited his natural curiosity, spirit of advancement, and drive to find ways to make things better throughout his life. Once he made a commitment to advance his sparks, there was no turning back, and, well, the rest is history!

"A Better Way": A Focal Point for Creative Action

When we are in the stage of advancing a spark, "a better way" becomes our focal point for creative action. A better way is something Jim Haudan, CEO and cofounder of Root Learning, has made one of the core values of his company. While Maumee, Ohio, may not be the first place you might look to as a hub for innovative learning methodologies, for the past fifteen years Haudan has worked with hundreds of top-level executives to help shape and deliver better ways of engaging leaders and developing and executing strategic plans. The results of their better ways have caught the attention of *Harvard Business Review* and *Fast Company*. Haudan says,

> We are challenged by the constant pursuit of a better way. Stimulating breakthrough ideas and coming up with excellent results is a habit that we cultivate that assumes that the way things are done today won't be good enough tomorrow. We are driven by the basic idea that if we can do better we should. The desire to advance our business and help others advance theirs is sparked by a process of constant searching, curiosity, discovery, change, and growth.

The Root Learning process of advancing learning and sparking creative solutions of change is unique in a billion-dollar industry that is over-reliant on standard methods of learning that passively impart knowledge and do little to get at underlying behaviors. Root Learning has brought together a diverse group of MBAs, artists, and programmers from all over the world to create an engaging process based on combining vivid imagery with key business realities to foster learning, promote understanding, and encourage more authentic behavior from senior management. The process is rooted in learning-map technology, where pictures literally tell the story that an organization wants to communicate to its employees. Typically these cartoonlike pictures captured on large posters tell stories about organization strategy and use a metaphor that quickly and easily communicates the intended message. This allows for dialogue among employees and learning retention is increased, resulting in not only more engaged employees, but employees who truly understand the organization's strategy on a more complex level. This is a creative, experiential, and fun approach to learning about organizational strategies and imperatives in a simple and safe way.

WE MUST NEVER BE AFRAID TO GO TOO FAR, FOR SUCCESS LIES JUST BEYOND.

—MARCEL PROUST, FRENCH NOVELIST

We have had the privilege of partnering with Jim Haudan and Root Learning on a number of consulting engagements where we witnessed the power of their unique approach to finding a better way. We worked with Pfizer Consumer Healthcare, an organization with a history of success and a very conservative leadership team. While Pfizer was committed to a better way, its leaders were not ready to adopt new ways of engaging their employee population. Open communication was foreign to the leadership group, let alone sharing the organization's stories, issues, and challenges, and at first the leaders resisted our attempts to use such an approach to stimulate change in their business and employee workforce.

However, the Pfizer team was faced with a need to quickly introduce their strategic plan to a 3,500-person global workforce. With the team at Root Learning, we were able to convince the Pfizer team of the importance of finding a better way to grow products, raise the level of customer experiences, and get at core management issues.

LEARNING MAP.

The combination of hard business facts and vivid images helped to create a forum of exchange and understanding. Within a record period of time this better way had 98 percent of the workforce aligned with the global strategic plan. In years past, Pfizer leaders would have relied on more traditional and slower forms of engaging employees on strategic plans. Instead, this new approach to engagement set up a platform for tremendous growth and innovation. Employees around the world were stimulated by this approach (along with other strategic initiatives) and the creative action that ensued is directly credited with the fact that they achieved their goal of becoming the number-one consumer health-care company as a result of joining forces with Johnson and Johnson.

Whether we are looking to push ourselves or others forward or are searching for a better way, the model of creative genius helps us understand how the five habits help us attract, attach to, and advance the sparks of inspiration in our lives. Whether we want to attract spark moments and create in our personal or professional lives, tapping into our creative genius through the use of these specific habits will get us there. It's not only a journey that will produce real results, but it's also fun, energizing, and guaranteed to reignite your passion and joie de vivre! So let's explore how we go about incorporating the five habits into our daily lives.

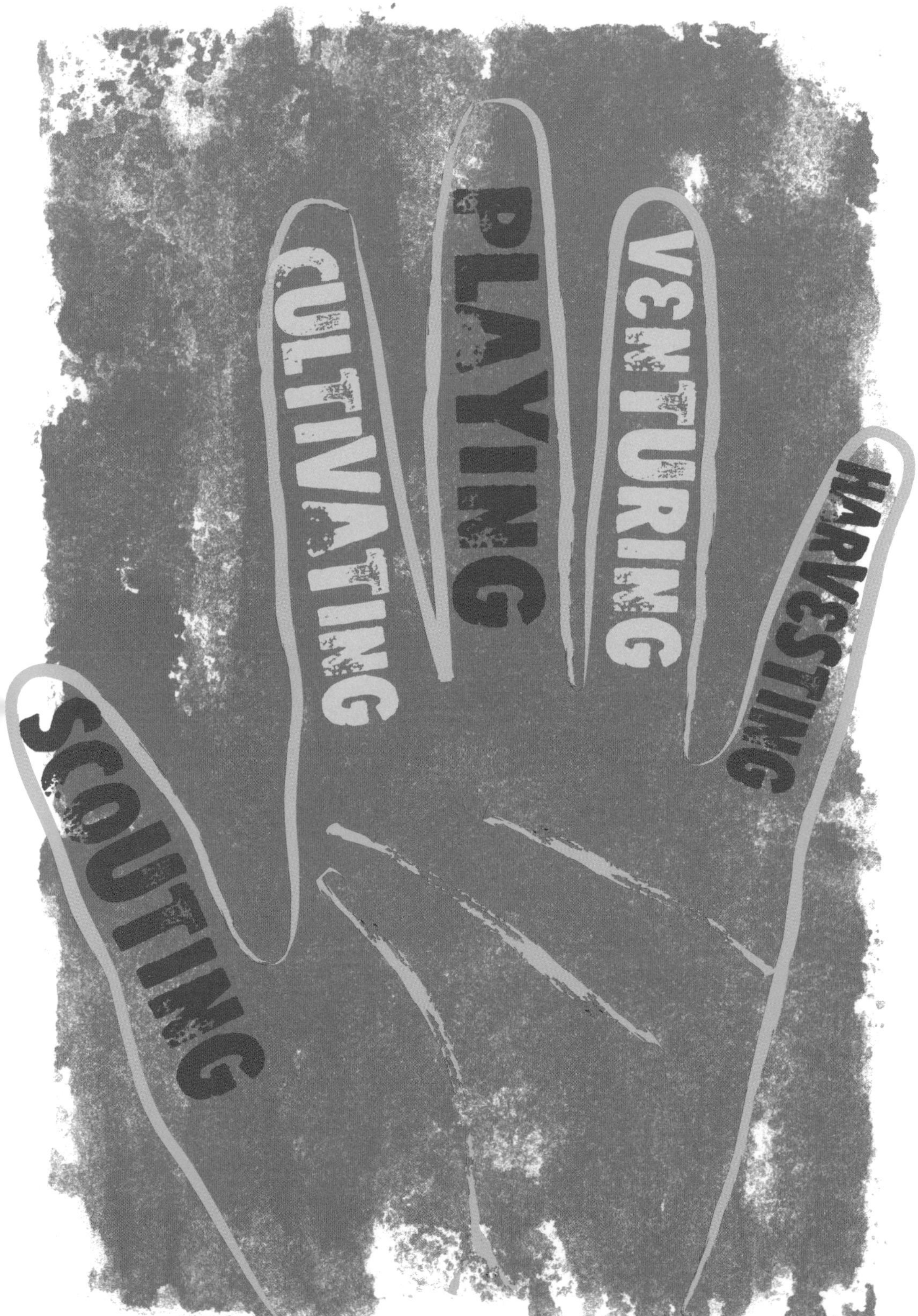
SCOUTING
CULTIVATING
PLAYING
VENTURING
HARVESTING

CHAPTER 3

Eyes Wide Open:
Scouting for Spark Moments

A few years ago we had the opportunity to work with Dave Raath, the head of innovation and product development for Johnson and Johnson's South Africa and Middle East division. While working with Dave to help him build a more innovative company culture, we had the opportunity to experience a group process they initiated and referred to as an "imbizo" group. *Imbizo* is the Zulu expression for "gathering," often used in political assemblies as a way of solving problems and discussing issues. "We use imbizo groups with an emphasis on creativity and innovation," says Dave. "From the shopkeeper to the members of the senior team, everyone is invited to come together and speak freely about creative business challenges and new ideas someone may have in growing customers and growing the business." The group generally meets on a weekly basis and on occasion brings in outside speakers and has refreshments as a way to entice people to attend. There are few, if any, ground rules other than to take in stimuli. Raath elaborates, "I believe it is important for our colleagues to feel more stimulated and these types of forums are one way of facilitating ideas or motivating someone to take action." With the imbizo group, the spotlight is on sparking the imagination, enlivening the creative spirit, and instilling a habit of creative action rather than focusing on the bottom line.

· ·

ENLIVEN YOUR CREATIVE SPRIT

What gets you stimulated? Is there a place you go to get centered or feel more "alive," a good thinking spot inside your home or in nature? When you have a challenge to solve, where do you do your best thinking? How do you do your best thinking? Do you like to journal? Do you like to talk it out with a trusted friend or colleague? Do you like to sit alone and contemplate?

What is it about the answers to the above questions that helps to get you stimulated and gives you a sense of enlivening your creative spirit?

Sketch how you enliven your creative spirit.

· ·

To facilitate our creative-genius potential, we can arrange activities in our daily lives so that we are exposed to and made conscious of many different forms of stimuli. The opportunity to scout abounds—we can scout everywhere and at all times by simply walking out the front door of our house or arranging an informal gathering of people. An amazing world of discovery awaits us each and every day, stimulating our senses and bringing color, experience, and sensation into full bloom. And in every experience or piece of evidence we bring to the surface through scouting, we hold the potential to spark our creative genius.

Through scouting, we can cultivate a sense of awe and wonder about the world and its people. Such a demeanor can arise, for example, simply by watching children tossing a Frisbee in the park or friends dining at a restaurant. With eyes wide open, the scout will notice the subtle differences between one experience and the next and discover the vital relationship between elements. For instance, in the case of a restaurant, the scout might discover how the food is acquired, prepared, delivered, and presented. The wonder and awe the scout experiences are the result of not

WHERE DO YOU DO YOUR BEST THINKING?

only taking in the basic dimensions of the restaurant experience—menus, plates, food—but also of the aesthetic qualities—lighting, expression, the demeanor of the waitstaff, the presentation of the food.

To help spark our creative genius, scouting should produce a stimulating effect on all of our senses. Mobility is necessary to practicing the habit of scouting to keep us active and alive with possibilities. When we are stimulated, there is a natural correlation between what we notice and what we feel. The basic premise behind scouting is to cultivate a rhythmic balance between curiosity, observation, absorption, inspiration, relevancy, and diversity. Fruitful scouting depends on the development of each of these elements.

On any given day one sensation alone can make the difference in how we feel and respond to the world. And on that day, that sensation may be just the spark we need to solve a problem, discover a unique idea, and enliven our creative spirit.

THE JoURNEY IS THE REWARD.

—CHINESE PROVERB

The Scout's Quest

Scouts are always moving from place to place in advance of everyone else. A scout is a person who is observing, inspecting, and discerning what's going on in her surroundings in order to obtain information and generate insight. As if on a hunt, the scout is looking to gather fresh intelligence that will inspire creative action. Perpetual seekers, scouts love the quest and the discovery of where their journey will take them. A scout moves with curiosity, energy, and anticipation and is devoted to observation and exploration. They are natural scanners with a keen ability to either see what no one else sees or to see the same things but derive new insights.

Scouts are curious in all sorts of ways. They are eager to learn and have the desire to get to the good stuff, the underlying cause of one thing or another. "Once you have nurtured curiosity the exploration of insights becomes contagious," says Marc Newberg, vice president of sales at HON. "Being curious helps me to keep myself open to the possibilities, and the more possibilities I am able to generate the more likely I am able to generate insights that will lead to creative solutions."

YOU CANNOT DEPEND ON YOUR EYES WHEN YOUR IMAGINATION IS OUT OF FOCUS.

—MARK TWAIN, AMERICAN HUMORIST, LECTURER, AND WRITER

Finding Inspiration

Andrea Weiss, CEO of Tabi International, whom we have known and worked with for many years, completely embodies the habits of a scout, particularly as they relate to finding and promoting inspirational ideas and actions. Through the many roles she plays in her life—including raising horses and serving on multiple boards—she is constantly on the lookout for information and experiences that will inspire her to come up with winning and innovative ways to help her and her organization compete in the marketplace.

> I find inspiration everywhere I go and in everything that I do. You just have to be willing to go out into the world with gusto and engage it. My inspiration will not come from one place, but many. Not from one type, but different types. I will get on a plane and look at an airline magazine

and tear out a story that is relevant or intriguing to something I may be engaged with at the time. It could also be a commercial or just a simple conversation that I may be having with someone else."

Early in her retail career, when she was the head of merchandising at Ann Taylor, Weiss was charged with retooling the entire field organization (the collection of employees who worked in all the stores across the country). With a clear understanding of the vision, Weiss set out to improve the experiences of customers who shop at an Ann Taylor store. She scoured each store for possibilities—for sparks that would help to reinvigorate what was at the time a somewhat haughty and out-of-touch organization.

Her epiphany—her spark moment—came when she toured various retail stores in Boulder, Colorado, with the district manager. Before touring one store, the district manager informed Weiss that they would be firing one of the store managers. Upon arriving, Weiss quickly scanned and noticed that the store was not well merchandised or organized—it lacked flair and pizzazz. Aware of the sensitive nature of the visit, Weiss hung back and decided to wander about the store while slowly making her way to the back room. In the back room, she found the district manager in conversation with the aforementioned store manager, whose fate was already decided. While the district manager talked, Weiss noticed a huge book with paper clippings and other objects jammed into its binding. Weiss pulled out the book and started to examine it. It belonged to the store manger who was moments away from being let go. The book contained hundreds of cards from lawyers, doctors, and businesspeople. The cards had business contact information and personal information such as their birthdays, clothing preferences, and color preferences. Enter spark moment. *Oh my God*, thought Weiss. *They are going to fire the woman who is the business, they are going to fire the business.* If they fired this manager, they were firing all of her connections—connections to rich opportunities, insights, and of course, customers. As if she were struck by a hundred volts of electrical charge, Weiss quickly experienced the inspiration she was searching for in her scouting activities.

THE KEY
TO FINDING
INSPIRATION
AND ACHIEVING
A CREATIVE
STEPPING-OFF POINT
IS TO DO SO WITH AN
OPEN MIND,
OPEN DOOR,
AND OPEN
HEART.

—Andrea Weiss,
CEO of Tabi International

By the time Weiss intervened, the manager was in tears from the news. Inspired by her discovery, Weiss insisted that while the manager may have been having difficulty in other aspects of running the store, it was clear she had talent and perhaps there was another way to use her and leverage her experience as represented by her business contact book. "This experience," Weiss recounted for us, "served as the pivotal moment and catalyst for creating a business model centered around a 'customer connection log' matched with a high degree of contact and customer knowledge." Weiss's scouting behavior saved the day, not only for the store manager, but also for the entire business.

IF YOU CHANGE
THE WAY YOU LOOK AT THINGS,
THE THINGS YOU
LOOK AT CHANGE.

—WAYNE W. DYER, AUTHOR AND LECTURER

The Conscious Observer

At first glance, a scout may appear to be a casual observer completely swept away with his own musings and not aware of anything else that is going on. In fact, the scout is very conscious of what is going on—just steadfastly focused. He is in a creative state of concentration, soaking up his experience and the subject of his observation. And the scout knows when to surface for air and relax his mind while opening it up for the spark moment. Once sparked, we begin to tap into the cycle of the creative genius on the path towards creating. Scouts take the time to savor the entire experience that they find themselves observing, nourishing their senses—they are seeing, touching, hearing, maybe smelling and tasting what is around them. This is all a means to experience and absorb the stimuli around them.

A scout is not searching or seeking perfection, just genuine experiences and phenomena. Scouts seek to describe a phenomenon as it unfolds before them. A skill developed by the best scouts is describing what *is* rather than interpreting *why* it is. Scouts describe what they see, what they hear, what they read (notice that you cannot *not* use your senses as a scout). Putting away any lens of interpretation is critical for the scout—it's about the process of immersing yourself in your environment, letting go of the outcomes. In other words, you don't know exactly when a spark moment will occur or your hard work will pay off, but you trust that it will as you are focused on the habit of scouting and immersing yourself in a stimulus, making yourself available to attract more and more of these moments.

DESCRIBING VS. INTERPRETING

Believe it or not, this is not as easy as it sounds. In our workshops on scouting, we explain, give examples of, and go over again and again the difference between describing something and interpreting the same thing. Inevitably and understandably, there are a few participants who, although they think they are being descriptive in their language, are in fact interpreting (or evaluating) what they are observing. So, as they say, practice makes perfect, so practice, practice, practice! Here are some examples:

Descriptive: She is tapping her cigarette box on the table.
Interpretive: She is nervous.
Descriptive: He is lying on the bed with his arm dangling off the side.
Interpretive: He is sick or he is asleep or he is dead.
Descriptive: Sally said, "I'm curious about the work you do."
Interpretive: Sally will quit her job and come work with me.

Can you sense the difference? Try it on your own at work or at home—it's a fun game with your family on a long drive or as an ice-breaker for a meeting.

Here's what you might try: Clip out different images from a magazine and ask your family or your colleagues to describe what they see. Watch to see how quickly they begin to interpret rather than describe the pictures. We've found that kids are typically better describers than us adults!

The skill of observation is developed through practice. And the more we practice our scouting habits, the more likely it is that we will have spark moments, make discoveries, and ultimately stimulate our creative genius. Only after a period of deep immersion and inner contemplation can we start to evaluate, wrestle with, and begin making interpretations of the clues and the spark moments we have found. Conscious observation is about curiosity, sensing, and suspending evaluation with a clear mind. Then new sparks are able to come forward, compelling us to either experiment (play) or venture upon the idea in a concrete way—in other words, we begin to court the idea as we become more attached to it.

CONSCIOUS OBSERVATION= CURIOSITY + SENSING + SUSPENDING

Isabel Briggs Myers and her mother, Katharine Cook Briggs, were responsible for the creation of what has become the most prolific and highly respected personality inventory of all time, the Myers-Briggs Type Indicator (MBTI). The instrument is an amazing example and result of conscious observation at work. From an early age, Isabel was known for her keen insight and ability to study people, developing a passionate interest in the differences in people from the moment she noticed she was herself different from her family.

With Isabels' bachelor's degree in political science as the extent of their combined higher education, the women brought to life a groundbreaking personality assessment now taken by at least two million people each year and translated into sixteen languages. Over a period of forty years, mother and daughter developed this instrument through simple astute observation of human behavior, and then later rigorous testing. They were drawn to the work of renowned psychologist Carl Jung, which sparked a passionate devotion to putting the theory of psychological type into practical circulation. With the onset of World War II, Briggs Myers realized that there was a severe manpower shortage as a result, and that because of this many women were entering the workforce for the first time. If she were to create a personality measurement tool to promote understanding and appreciation of human differences, it would be an invaluable gift to helping these women—and all people—choose careers and jobs that best matched their preferences and other personality traits.

Briggs Myers was attuned to her environment through her well-cultivated scouting habits. She was able to identify the behaviors, issues, and dramas that were unfolding right before her own eyes, and she gathered this information to help others make informed decisions about job choices. It was because of her observations that Briggs Myers was able to attach to the spark moments through which innovative solutions were given the fertile ground to emerge.

· ·

BRIGGS MYERS'S PERSPECTIVE ON HUMAN BEHAVIOR

"What Is to Be Desired?" by Isabel Briggs Myers

- **Self-respect:** To be part of the solution, not part of the problem
- **Love:** To love the human beings who mean the most to me, and contribute to their lives if I can
- **Peace of Mind:** To avoid mistakes that make me regret the past or fear the future
- **Involvement:** Always to be tremendously interested
- **Understanding:** To incorporate the things, people, and ideas that happen to me into a coherent concept of the world
- **Freedom:** To work at what interests me most, with minimum expenditure of time and energy on nonessentials

· ·

Total "Ob-sorp-vation"

Like a dedicated anthropologist, a scout completely immerses herself in her "field work" and will rarely come up for air until she is satisfied with what she has found. While researching and preparing for writing this book, we met and interviewed several scouts. One, a school psychologist in Western Ohio named John Biltz, stood out because of his passion and commitment to helping special-needs children. In this role, John has to straddle the difficult and sometimes heart-wrenching challenges of how best to empower a learning- or developmentally challenged child and his or her parents in order to provide that child with an optimal and fulfilling life and learning experience. John told us about some of the many profound experiences he has had, with children whose difficulties range from autism to attention deficit disorders. When we asked him what he does to get stimulated to produce a plan of action that creatively meets the needs of the student, the parent, and the school, he replied,

> I find myself coming up with my most creative ideas when I am totally immersed in a topic, doing research and reading about something related to the topic. When I totally immerse myself I am locked and loaded, so to speak. I push everything away until I am completely saturated like a cloud that is ready to burst and open up. It is during this time of saturation where I suspend my immersion, observation, and study, and then consciously I give myself permission to think about something else.

Clearly, as a scout, John has learned to immerse himself to gather all the intelligence and information he needs and then, once he is done scouting, "gives himself permission" to let go and focus on other things. Often scouts will spend a lot of time hunting, searching, and looking out for clues, and at some point during the exploration process, they will suspend their activity and let go for a brief period in order to relax the mind and open themselves up for spark moments.

BY LETTING IT GO, IT ALL GETS DONE. THE WORLD IS WON BY THOSE WHO LET IT GO.

—LAO TZU, CHINESE TAOIST/PHILOSOPHER

One night while watching *Inside the Actors Studio*, we saw Robin Williams being interviewed by the phlegmatic host, James Lipton. Well, actually it was more like watching a comedy routine, with Williams buzzing from one improvisation to another, keeping the audience in stitches while sharing some of his story of becoming an actor and comedian. One of the many things that struck us was how Robin Williams described his approach to creation and improvising ideas and situations. As an only child growing up in a middle-class home in Detroit, Michigan, Williams learned to study people and spark his imagination by completely immersing himself in the subject matter and experience of observing others. With an elongated and punctuated sound on the letters *a* and *b,* he said, "I *absorb* myself completely into the moment and experience that I am a part of." We liked his description and it sparked for us a fresh way of looking at the process of scouting as not just a static or passive activity of observing, but also an involvement in the experience itself. By allowing yourself to be completely caught up in and absorbed by the experience of watching, searching, and listening, you allow your imagination to run free.

THE WORLD IS BUT A CANVAS TO THE IMAGINATION.

—Henry David Thoreau, American author
and philosopher

So, in the spirit of imagination and creativity, we've coined a new word that we use in our workshops to help participants understand the habit of scouting by joining the words *observation* and *absorption* together—ob-sorp-vation. Ob-sorp-vation means that when we seek stimulus and insight, we must not only watch what is going on, but we must also permit ourselves on occasion to be completely swept up into the moment of the experience that we are observing, allowing ourselves to become a part of the drama.

While touring a private school and observing how they encourage their students to be creative, we noticed that the teachers begin with some type of phenomenon, for example, something happening in nature that each student must observe. The students are then encouraged to take their observations into a deeper form of inner contemplation, wrestle with it, and seriously immerse themselves in it before describing what they see and experience. Once a foundation of observation and absorption (ob-sorp-vation) into a phenomenon is established, this school believes possibilities will open up and new discoveries will be made.

To attract spark moments and free our senses, scouts will immerse themselves in a source of data or experience in order to unearth something a casual observer or examiner may not have noticed. Fleeting glances will not suffice for the scout who seeks rich insight and possibilities. He will observe and absorb new information with gusto and seek out the points of a situation that may have been overlooked or even misunderstood.

A Need for Diversity

As important as it is to be really absorbed in a particular topic, it is equally important to consider stimulus, data, and information from diverse sources to enrich your field of observation. Creative ideas are never generated through homogeneous sources. Whenever we are working with a client or group through our seminars we encourage them to go out into the world and scan the world for possibilities with an intent to obtain diverse information. If you rely on the same sources of data and experience to stimulate creative action, eventually the observations and insights you make will be similar and stale. Scouting is about encouraging people to search for clues from different sources in order to stimulate new, fresh ideas, ones that other people would not have generated. The trick is to eventually see how this insight might be applied to your specific situation and made relevant—but not quite yet. Right now, it's all about scouting.

Whether you are working in an organization that is under constant pressure to discover the next big thing (as most are), or you personally want to make a difference in this world, you need to make sure you are not only looking in different places from your competitors or other people, but that you are also looking in the same places with different eyes and asking different questions.

THE **REAL** VOYAGE OF **DISCOVERY** CONSISTS NOT IN SEEKING **NEW LANDSCAPES** BUT IN HAVING **NEW EYES.**

—MARCEL PROUST, FRENCH NOVELIST

In order to produce unique ideas and develop creative solutions to change, you must develop a keen set of observation, exploration, and discovery skills. Observing behavior or studying consumers in different environments with a different set of lenses, so to speak, is necessary for creative success.

We recently worked with a large food manufacturer to improve their scouting abilities in order to generate fresh new insights about savory, healthy, convenient food items. Specifically, the head of new product development (NPD) approached us to help teach sophisticated marketers and designers basic ethnographic techniques. These individuals were very experienced with following consumer behaviors and often used other firms to canvass insights. However, in the opinion of the NPD head, they were disconnecting with fundamental observations of consumers that had as much if not more fertile possibilities for innovations relevant to their marketplace. Aptly, the NPD head said, "I really want them to both witness and develop the habits of perception and observation."

In working with this group, we presented them with a challenge and encouraged them to study consumers in a variety of settings, not just supermarkets or convenience stores, where typically their products would be stocked. Instead, we had them look at what we call alternative spots to help spark insights. For example, we had them go to tanning salons, fitness centers, and hotels to observe and understand in general how people maintain their health and adopt healthy habits. It was through these kinds of diverse experiences that their marketers got more in touch with what consumers value. They were also able to get an idea about different kinds of customer experiences and to infer what matters most in terms of package-design solutions and alternative channels of distribution. And, of course, they had fun with an experience that opened their minds to all sorts of amazing possibilities.

The aim of traditional organizations is to lead employees into particular functions and fields of knowledge—marketing, sales, and research and development. However, a scout has the opposite aim—she strives to transform diverse fields of knowledge into patterns and forms and ways that encourage more holistic methods of making sense of information. To keep their creative juices flowing, scouts are called upon to gather insight from many diverse points of view.

A Focus on Relevance

However, scouts must balance diversity with relevance. A scout will be attracted to situations, people, and circumstances that are tied to a particular problem or need she is seeking to solve or fulfill. To spark our creative genius to help solve a problem, we must be intentional and conscious about what we might be seeking, where we search and how we make sense of the things we are observing, studying, and absorbing.

"When you begin to hone in on what's relevant and what's not spoken," suggests Jim Haudan of Root Learning, "you are able to discover things that may be 'undiscussable.'" Root Learning knows how important it is to immerse yourself in relevant context to put yourself in the right creative state of mind. Haudan, who began his career as a football coach, says that to stimulate creative ideas you need to make your observations relevant. "As a coach, it was always important for me to make a connection to my players and explain the playbook and execution of a particular play in ways that they would understand." Haudan also says, "If a comedian is really connecting with people and making them laugh, it's very likely because he or she is picking up on the cues and energy of the audience and consequently translating his routine into something that is relevant."

In our own work, when we are speaking to an audience, conducting a workshop, or consulting with a client, if we do not scan our environment and make relevant observations or react in a way that makes a connection with the audience, then we will fail to spark the necessary energy to form a creative relationship with the audience.

Relevance is pivotal to how you engage yourself and others, and to how you influence perceptions. However, a word of caution: while we certainly want to balance relevance with diversity, we don't want to do it prematurely. At the early stages of scouting, it's all about diverging—going out and about to many places, perhaps without knowing exactly why or how where you are exploring is relevant—and that's okay. In fact, it's critical. But at some point during your scouting you may need to make some choices based upon why you are scouting in the first place. The trick is to do enough diverse scouting without putting limitations on yourself but know when to shift the focus to scouting in areas that might be more relevant to your purpose. For example, if you are scouting to find a new medical solution that helps livestock stay healthy, relevant and diverse scouting may include such things as visiting cattle farms, veterinarians, or even pet psychics! As you begin to focus on relevancy (after giving enough time for diversity) you may determine that heading to a fashion retailer that specializes in leather products isn't relevant enough for your particular purpose—you'd rather spend your time elsewhere. Taking into consideration the time, effort, cost, and the like become factors to help you make choices about relevancy related to your scouting efforts. Bottom line, when you are scouting, trust your judgment and determine the balance you need between obtaining diverse and relevant stimulus.

Scouting in Action

The process of scouting helps to nurture our desire to be curious and encourages us to be in the moment through a process of observation and deep absorption. It also offers us the opportunity to gather diverse and relevant information that can inspire our creative genius. The more we scout, the more possibilities we open ourselves up to. Scouting activity brings us more fully to our creative state by helping us to stay in touch with our external environment, our inner awareness, and the consciousness of others and their experiences.

YOU KNOW YOU'RE A SCOUT WHEN . . .

For each of the given statements below, please circle the one that is most like you, most of the time.

- I'm insatiably curious. In fact, Curious George is my hero.
- I'm indifferent to what goes on around me . . . I could care less. "Whatever" is my motto.

- I love to get out and about and have new experiences.
- I'd rather sit home and stare at the boob tube.

- Diversity to me means "Wow, lots to learn from."
- Diversity to me means "Ugh, lots to learn from."

- I look at things and think "What could be, what if, how might I?"
- I look at things and think "I can't, I won't, I've tried before."

- I respect and engage with others whose opinions are radically different from mine.
- Different opinions? No way, not me . . . it's all about conformity.

- I feel it's possible to describe what I see, hear, and read as is . . . with no interpretation of why it is.
- Not a chance. It's impossible to be completely descriptive . . . there's always a bit of interpretation to information we receive.

- I often say things like "Anything is possible if you put your mind to it."
- I often say things like "Not everything is possible . . . I'm a realist."

- I'm more about living in the moment with each and every experience.
- I'm more worried about getting it done—I barely have any moments.

Okay, by now it may be obvious that the more first statements you circled, the more of a scout you are. Now, this doesn't mean that if you circled some second statements, there is no way for you to become a wonderful scout; in fact, just the opposite. You can change the way you approach things and cultivate the specific habits of a scout.

So how do we work to actively become scouts? Following are the first steps.

1. Determine the challenge you are facing and put it in the form of a possibility-oriented question: *How might I . . . What if I . . .*

2. Brainstorm different ways of finding stimulus: Where might you go? What might you do? What might you read? What might you try? Be sure to think of diverse things and be open to including things you may never have considered before.

3. Grab a pencil and notebook and get moving! Record your observations—what you see, what you hear, what you read—and don't worry too much about what it means or why it is, just record.

4. As you are ob-sorp-vating, be conscious of spark moments and write them down! Be sure to stay curious and open-minded and try to see things differently. Take on the persona of an anthropologist, and allow yourself to get inspired. Go deeper into the experience by trying out the people or events you are observing . . . try not to get into trouble on this one!

5. As you are out and about, pick up artifacts along the way to remind you of ideas or of the journey itself.

6. Have fun! This is part of the experience. Relax, enjoy, and soak it all up!

At the end of these scouting experiences, take a look at what you've collected in the form of artifacts and observations and gather them all together—we like to make collages of all the "stuff" and step back to take it all in. Ask yourself, "What were my spark moments and what do those have to tell me? What did I learn? What stories do I have to tell? What patterns do I see emerging from this information? What might this mean? How is it relevant to my initial challenge or question?"

Taking these steps and asking these questions will get you on the path to becoming a scout and stimulating your creative genius.

TIPS FOR SCOUTING

- Get out and about: instead of sitting at your desk this morning, go to a local coffee shop and watch people (if you need a permission slip for your boss, send us an e-mail!).
- Take a new route to work. Whether you drive or commute via public transportation, go a new way. You never know what you might see.
- Pick up a magazine that you would never read normally: if you're not one for sailing, pick up a sailing magazine; if you don't get into race car driving, pick up a magazine about racing. You might be surprised by what sparks are triggered for you when you look at different things.
- Look at things differently. Maybe you've got the "same old, same old" presentation or work product to get ready for your boss. Instead of looking at it as a chore and a drag, use this as an opportunity to "change the way you look at things." Try adding your own expression to your work or go to a new location to do the work or grab a latte and get some extra stimulation for trudging through!
- Play the "opposite game." Look at things from the opposite point of view; take on and argue the opposite of what you think. For example, if you are for one political candidate, think about his/her opponent and pretend that you are for that candidate. What might you learn from this experiment?
- Catch yourself evaluating. Next time you find yourself evaluating something, stop yourself and just observe. Don't give in to the temptation to immediately judge something as good or bad, just let it be.
- Be curious. Ask why, ask why not.
- Try a new sport.
- Take a vacation in a location you've never been to before.
- When faced with a situation, first ask yourself, "How do I feel?" Get attuned to your senses and feelings to arrive at some new insights.
- Journal, journal, journal. Buy a new pen and nice journal and capture your observations in any and all situations!

CHAPTER 4

Spaces and Places: Cultivating Spark Moments

When we were in the process of researching, conducting interviews, and generally getting organized to write this book, we would often frequent different places to stimulate our senses and look to cultivate spark moments. We would hang out at the Art Café, one of our favorite coffee houses in our neighborhood, which has a cozy half-moon-shaped seat that everyone covets. Behind the seat is a bay window that on most days provides abundant natural light and thermal energy that can help the person sitting there feel stimulated and warm, especially on a cold winter's day. It's the best seat in the house and a great place to create.

The ambiance at the Art Café and similar establishments helps to put us in a proper mental and physical state in which to reflect, converse, and brainstorm. From the fragrant candles in the bathroom to the soft music in the background and the attentive and slightly chatty waitstaff, the entire setting primes our energy for creating. It is in a place like this that we appreciate the importance of environment and recognize situations that make us feel more energized and excited.

We relish the natural light and the warm and personal environment, but you may find that a dark café with cement floors and a surly staff is a better working environment for you. There's no "right" for everyone. We each have preferences. What is important is that the location you choose gives you the right level of energy to create.

LOVE OF BEAUTY IS TASTE. THE CREATION OF BEAUTY IS ART.

—RALPH WALDO EMERSON,
AMERICAN POET AND LECTURER

In addition to the café, our local library is also a frequent haunt, especially when we need a quieter space to be more reflective and concentrate deeply on our research and writing. On occasion we may step into a busy café thinking we need high energy only to realize that we are distracted and prefer a space that is quiet and allows us to concentrate. When you go to a place like a library you have access to many stimulating things: people of all ages to watch, windows to sit in, books and magazines to thumb through, the Internet to explore, music to listen to, movies to watch, and more. Any of these things can stimulate your creative genius. The trick in cultivating spark moments is to choose the right space that balances your need for concentration versus your need for high energy. If your creative task requires you to meditate, then a place that is still and quiet may be perfect. If, on the other hand, you need to encourage people to play, having a noisier and funkier space may be the right environment.

STIMULATING SPACES AND PLACES

Think about your own spaces and places—where you live, where you work, where you visit. What is it about each of these places that is stimulating for you? What's not stimulating, and what might you do to change it?

Often we don't need to make a major change like move to a new house, community, etc. (and many times, even when we want to, it might not be immediately feasible). But you can do small things to make your spaces and places more stimulating.

For example, our home has a wonderful view of the river, so we organize our furniture to maximize our ability to take in this view in any way we can. We also have cozy "nook" spaces within our small abode that serve as mini-escapes for thinking, reading, and meditating. And when all else fails, we get out of those spaces altogether and try something new—a local coffee shop, a park—anything that will get us in a different, more stimulating space and place. Think about these questions and take action today to get more stimulated:

- How might you stimulate your current work or home environment?
- Where might you go to get a change of space or place?
- When I really need time to think, where's the best space or place for me to go? How might I get there more regularly?

Environment as a Creative Catalyst

When a fruit ripens, it becomes more edible and sweet tasting. Before it ripens, it will likely be too bitter or too starchy to enjoy. Overripe, a fruit will be too mushy and taste rotten. A ripe piece of fruit emits a gas, ethylene, that causes the fruit to soften and taste sweet. Ethylene increases the cellular activity of specific enzymes in fruit and other fresh-cut products.

The process of being stimulated and cultivating spark moments with your creative genius is similar to a fruit or vegetable ripening. If your environment is rich with stimulating sensations or creative enzymes, then the conditions are ripe for spark moments. The environment serves as a catalyst for creative sparks and action. But unlike fruits and vegetables, we can affect our environments to help produce the reactions we seek. For example, music is a terrific way to change your state of mind. By simply putting on your favorite songs you can change the way you feel or recall a memory that will help you feel more relaxed or energized.

MUSIC: PRIMITIVE STIMULUS

In Dr. Daniel Levitin's book, *This Is Your Brain on Music*, he states that our brains are hardwired to understand music because "it preceded language as a mode of communication." In other words, Levitin says, "When we hear music, not speech, it stimulates these very ancient, primitive parts of the brain that are below the level of conscious thought."

Using high-tech equipment, Levitin can detect the specific areas of the brain that are stimulated by various types of music. For example, Levitin found that when subjects listened to Mozart, the place where the brain interprets pitch, timbre, and rhythm was activated. When subjects listened to Eminem, however, the regions responsible for language were accessed. So whether you load Chopin or Chicago into your iPod, it represents one powerful way to stimulate your creative state of mind.

Some environments may either inhibit or activate our creative genius. For example, the lighting may be too bright or too dark. Or perhaps you have come across a meeting space with big and clunky furniture better suited to a flea market than to a creative brainstorm. The type of space and the type of place will make a difference and affect your ability to cultivate spark moments. To activate and sustain your creative genius, choose a space or place that is a unique expression of who you are and that evolves

CULTIVATING

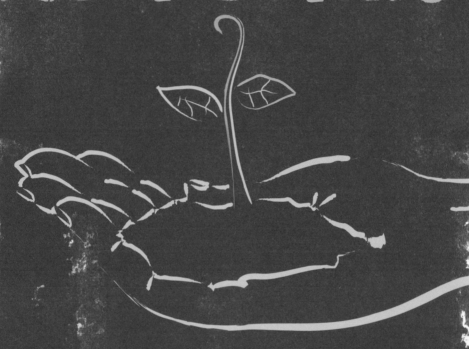

CREATIVE
SPACES AND PLACES
FERTILE CONDITIONS
PROPER ENVIRONMENT
TO FLOURISH

over time to meet your needs. Start by understanding the spaces and places that fit best and provide you with the ease and inspiration for cultivating spark moments.

THE IMAGINATION IS HOW THINGS GET DONE. YOU HAVE TO CULTIVATE CREATIVITY.

—RUSSELL SIMMONS, ENTREPRENEUR

Not long ago we were working with Tom, a head of consumer marketing for a health-care company responsible for generating innovations to promote healthy habits in the home. Tom was interested in increasing people's awareness of how to maintain their health. His findings were usually not very stimulating or, as he put it, "groundbreaking." Generally he would assemble a group of consumers around a rectangular conference table, set up a couple of flip charts, and bring in some sample products. Though he had the essentials for conducting a focus group, his setup was hardly the recipe for stimulating big ideas. Every now and then, because of his enthusiastic nature, Tom was able to tease out a kernel or two of an idea from a consumer.

After months of disappointment and trying new approaches, Tom and his organization decided to redesign one of the stodgy conference rooms to make it look more like a comfortable home. They added funky furniture with soft, vibrant pillows. They brought in more plants, more artwork for the walls, and cool lamps and better lighting that they could manipulate to alter the mood. In addition, they had a refrigerator stocked full of healthy snacks and beverages and an inviting island table in the shape of a kidney that made it easy for people to sit, talk, and sip their lattes. Dubbed the "consumer playground," the room became the perfect place for putting consumers in the proper mental state from which to spark ideas and originate useful, insightful feedback. By simply changing the atmosphere of one of their conference rooms, Tom and his organization developed an environment suited to generate insights about consumer behavior in the home.

DOGS NEED STIMULATING ENVIRONMENTS TOO!

The January 2005 issue of the *Journal of Neurobiology of Aging* reports on an interesting study conducted by researchers from the University of Toronto and the University of California.

They found that a combination of a more stimulating environment and more nutritious diet (with fruits, vegetables, and vitamins) improved brain function in older dogs.

This cognitive stimulation included things like the ability to interact with other dogs (socialization), getting exercise at least twice a week, and having access to novel toys.

The implication for humans seems obvious. If dogs, who engage in complex cognitive strategies like humans and have more complicated brains than most other animals, react so positively to stimulating environments, wouldn't we have improved brain function and learning in more stimulating environments as well?

So, just for fun (and in the name of research), go out and socialize more often, get exercise, and buy yourself a new toy! Seriously, get yourself into some different, stimulating environments and see what happens. We're convinced you will see dramatic benefits. And do let us know what happens—we'd like to hear your story.

The Power of Aesthetics in Your Spaces and Places

Derived from the Greek word *aisthetike,* the word "aesthetic" first pertained to the study of perceptions, until the eighteenth-century German philosopher Alexander Baumgarten linked it to "the science of beauty" and how things are appreciated via the senses. As our creativity blossoms in our childhood, we become more and more attuned to the creative factors that produce sensations of awe and excitement. Why is it that we prefer one color over another, one dress or shirt over another? How does pulling on your favorite pair of jeans make you feel?

We define aesthetics as the important and sometimes little-noticed lever that creates the vibe and hopefully produces the sparks that inspire the desired creative outcome or context. Sometimes subtle and sometimes in your face, aesthetics have the potential to provoke a range of feelings, such as excitement, laughter, discomfort, sadness, and contemplation. As you think about cultivating your creative genius, think about the vibe or sensation you wish to produce with outcomes that involve more than yourself. If what you seek is a high esprit de corps in your team, then post images of high-performing teams, take your team to a sporting event that requires complex teamwork, or place various physical objects around to remind you and your team of the importance of cooperation and communication. Once again, the environment you shape or choose should match the vibe or sensation you wish to impart.

While beauty may be in the eye of the beholder and personal taste may differ from one person to the next, it is important to be conscious of how the aesthetics in your environment stimulate and spark your creative genius—or not. By turning your attention to the aesthetic, you naturally focus on the moment and sensations that spark your creative side. It's no surprise, then, that while you are lathering up in the shower, taking a walk along one of your favorite paths, or hearing a great song, you feel an increase in energy and freshness that excites your senses and opens you up to the possibilities.

"I love to use my drive time to clear my head out and get rid of the clutter," says Shelly Walsh, head of design at Tabi International, a leader in women's fashion in Canada. "I also like to put on music to stimulate my senses, or I will rent old movies such as *Casablanca* or *Roman Holiday* if I need to put myself in the mode of thinking 'classic' . . . when you need to be creative you need to immerse yourself in the beauty of your surroundings and use every available prop, form, or sensation to spark new ideas."

Whether creating big bonfires at her family's farm, where they invite their community over for Christmas cheer, or riding a train across the wilderness of Canada, Walsh says, "You can learn best and have nothing to lose when you put yourself in a pleasant environment—I like wood, water, warmth; they give me confidence, pleasure, and security. I am better able to concentrate, take risks, and have harmony when I pay close attention to my experiences and environment."

EVERYTHING HAS BEAUTY, BUT NOT EVERYONE SEES IT.
—CONFUCIUS, CHINESE PHILOSOPHER

Pay close attention to all the moments you savor and to the things that fully engage your creative senses. Once you have acknowledged these elements, you can be more deliberate in how you set up an environment with aesthetics that will connect with your needs. For example, if you need the same place to elicit high-energy brainstorming as well as time to concentrate, include aesthetic touches that evoke motivating and exciting sensations as well as those that suggest softer, more subtle sensations.

The more we connect ourselves to aesthetic conditions of success, the more we are able to make creative thinking and action a part of everything we do. And the more we make these connections, the more we increase our sense of good taste and appreciation for the artistic nature of environment and how it can keep us sparking with possibilities and feeling stimulated.

A few years ago we helped a Norwegian pharmaceutical company kick off its innovation effort in an unusual place. After we coached the leaders on the importance of having the right environment, they landed on a slightly weird but very appropriate place called the Mini Bottle Museum. This museum housed a collection of thousands upon thousands of the miniature bottles that contain alcohol and come with a mixer when you order a drink on a flight. The Mini Bottle Museum offered a strange but nonetheless perfect atmosphere that the team wanted to have at their innovation meeting. The leaders wanted to signal that innovation is not business as usual, that thinking weird is not only just okay, but that it is necessary to produce big results. After years of flat sales they were ready to shake things up, and they thought the museum would be the perfect place to stimulate out of the box—or should we say out of the bottle?—thinking. And it worked! Rather than drinking its sorrows away because of a flat market, this team achieved unprecedented growth. The Mini Bottle Museum offered an appropriately eclectic atmosphere and set the tone for the Norwegian team, and within months, the team had stimulated double-digit growth in a market hovering at 2 percent. Many of the team members said that had they not gone to such a facility they would not have dared to generate big ideas. The aesthetics of that environment helped put the team in a very creative and daring state of mind that was both comfortable and provocative.

Aligning Outcome and Aesthetics

One of our favorite places to capture and store up sparks is on the eastern shores of Long Island, New York, in a town called Amagansett. Home to a collection of professionals, celebrities, artists, and weekend vacationers, Amagansett boasts some of the most elegant beaches and picturesque sunrises and sunsets on the earth. Besides its eclectic inhabitants and natural

THE BEST AND
MOST BEAUTIFUL
THINGS IN THE WORLD
CANNOT BE SEEN OR
EVEN TOUCHED.
THEY MUST BE FELT
WITH THE HEART.

—HELEN KELLER, AMERICAN AUTHOR, ACTIVIST,
AND LECTURER

beauty, the town offers plenty of stimuli to soak up. We often come to this place to relax and write.

In addition to the crashing waves, salty sea air, and sandy beaches, one of the important but not always appreciated features of the shore is the many dunes that serve as a natural barrier between the mighty Atlantic and the posh homes of that area. These small, undulating hills grace the perimeter of the mainland and are the subject of many landscapes painted by local artists. Not only are the dunes pretty to look at and a source of inspiration for many, they also have the practical functions of protecting the shores from erosion and providing a hospitable environment for plant and animal life. In short, they are both aesthetically satisfying and functionally important—they represent both pleasure and purpose.

To cultivate spark moments and your creative genius, you need spaces—like the dunes—that are pleasing and purposeful. There are two important factors to consider when choosing the right place and creating the right space in order to be most creative: your desired outcomes and time.

Desired Outcomes

Determining your desired outcomes is part of your creative challenge or goal. What are you working on or wanting to change that requires creative energy and action? Are you stuck and, like our client and friend David, feeling creatively empty? Are you struggling to find a new formula or therapy for healing? Do you need to come up with a compelling and more highly differentiated advertising campaign? Are you stuck in a relationship that is not satisfying? Are you bored with your job? These are just a few problems that may require creative thinking and action. Every day we are faced with a myriad of challenges and opportunities in which we can exercise and apply our creative genius. The trick is to get into the proper state and place to let our creative muscles flex in ways that yield the desired results—sparks and insights that lead to innovative solutions or inspired action.

Let's face it, we are usually more stimulated when we are with a bunch of energetic people or in a more interesting spot, such as one that has loads of artwork or comfortable furnishings or nifty tools we can play with. When we are clear about our creative goals, we can make better choices about the spot that will best stimulate our creative genius. Depending on your desired outcome or challenge, you may need a place that inspires or a place that provides focus. If you need new, fresh input, go to a place where you can be inspired or a place that you have never been before: somewhere that is foreign and requires you to listen and observe more. Or change your existing space through pictures, color, words, and other elements that will alter your vibe or let you feel more comfortable. If what you need is concentration to work on an existing idea or break through a block, choose a place or create a space that allows you to retreat and focus and be free from distraction. Seclusion permits you to suspend thoughts about other matters and helps to sweep away any clutter in your mind that may inhibit your creative genius.

It's possible, however, to go over the top arranging the aesthetics portion of your environment. You can create a beautiful, exciting environment, but if it is not appropriately aligned and attuned to your desired creative outcomes, then you will not necessarily succeed in stimulating the right sparks there. In the beginning stages of building a more innovative culture, some of the clients we have worked with have fallen into this trap. Once, we were asked to speak to an executive team for a bank off-site, and the team was so enthusiastic about sending a message about innovative action and implementation that they pulled out all the stops for the meeting. From dry ice and inspirational posters to skits, music, and team-building activities, the agenda dictated a lot of fun, but the team didn't meet the goal of the meeting, because too much was going on simultaneously. In short, the aesthetic nature of the meeting was misaligned with the team's desired outcomes. We applauded the team's creativity, but we also reminded them that being creative and developing creative environments for creativity's sake will not guarantee creative sparks and opportunities.

However, if you focus only on the outcome and downplay the aesthetics, you will also probably not inspire creative action. Take, for example, the game of baseball. If you attend a professional baseball game at a stadium but there are no refreshments being sold, the experience of watching the game will not be as pleasant. Part of what we crave is the beauty of the experience—the green grass, the peanuts, and concessionaires selling cold beer. While the players may still play their game on the field (outcome), your experience of the event will not be as stimulating without the aesthetics (cold beer and peanuts). The conditions for sparks are best stimulated when we factor in both the creative outcomes and the appropriate aesthetic conditions needed to produce the ideal sensations.

Tools and structures are also important in achieving your desired outcomes. Whether you are in discovery mode, playing with concepts, or evaluating options, you need the proper set of tools and structures to generate stimulating and creative sparks. An anthropologist without a journal or an executive team without a process for brainstorming decisions cannot efficiently stimulate creative thought and action. You simply cannot produce big ideas or solve problems creatively if you don't have the right tools or approaches to meet your creative challenge.

Time

The second factor that relates to aesthetics and outcomes is time. Time and space go hand in hand. If you are not constrained by time, you will have many more options for spaces and places that foster and focus your creative energy. Being constrained by time, however, does not necessarily mean you can ignore your environment. It is easy to use time as an excuse not to cultivate your creative genius. Some of the most creative people we know demonstrate the same thoroughness in ordinary tasks as they do in creative activity. Part of how effective you are at cultivating your creative genius is how you use your time and the extent to which you balance structured time, when you need to be focused, with unstructured time, when you can really let your mind wander. Regardless of whether the time you have is structured or unstructured, there are always simple and effective ways to cultivate and sustain a stimulated and creative state of mind. For example, playing with a simple Koosh ball, dressing casually and getting out of stuffy business attire, or playing music in the background can all keep you in a proper creative mind-set. Take time to create the space and add the small personal twists that inspire you and allow you to work fluidly, despite the constraints of your structure. It fosters the right environment for cultivating your creative genius, and it's easy!

Weaving Creative Conditions into Everything You Do

Saori is an art of weaving by hand that is dedicated to creative expression and development. Saori weavers often profess that anyone can do it, regardless of skill and knowledge. The *sa* of Saori is the first syllable of *sai*, a Japanese word meaning "everything has its own individual expression and art form." And the *ori* means "weaving and improvisation from the heart, with no preconceived idea."

Infinite designs may unfold in Saori using multiple colors and threads, each more beautiful than the other. The philosophy behind Saori weaving is to release one's creative genius in harmony with the loom, the thread, and the energy of the weaver. Often used for therapeutic purposes, Saori is said to open people's minds, helping them realize their creative potential.

The philosophy of Saori suggests that we are all creative beings and that the power of this weaving process (which often includes loose threads and accidentally skipped threads) can help us to feel more creative and confident to experiment or take risks. In other words, cultivating your creative genius is somewhat like weaving. The weaver represents the creator. The loom represents the spaces and the places and the tools we utilize in order to create. The design is the result of the weaving (creating) we do. The more you weave and experiment and accept that "accidents" are a part of the creative cultivation process, the more you are open to the possibilities and apt to create and be creative. Naturally, organizations struggle with the concept of accepting accidents, because they expect perfection and exactness. In certain circumstances, such as surgery or manufacturing products, precision is obviously key. You cannot afford to make mistakes when someone's life is on the line. However, if you are required to think big, solve problems, or inspire others to perform at high levels, then by all means, encourage "weaving" of all sorts. Out of the process some wonderful, unexpected results can emerge. The soul of cultivating spark moments is serendipity—the effect by which one accidentally discovers something fortunate, especially while seeking something else entirely.

A few years ago, we had the privilege to work with Pfizer Consumer Healthcare to help them become more creative and innovative. Over a period of time Pfizer produced many innovations through intentional cultivation. While the results were not rapid at first and mistakes were made along the way, the overall results were dramatic. Listerine Pocket Paks, the nifty and effective little strips of Listerine that instantly dissolve in your mouth, is a great example of intentional cultivation. Pfizer was very keen on changing the form of the mouthwash Listerine into a more portable form, because marketing and consumer insights suggested that consumers were looking for convenient solutions for keeping their mouths fresh and free of germs. After all, we all want clean mouths, but how many people do you see lugging a large bottle of mouthwash around in their purse or car? It just isn't practical. After many years of experimentation and encouraging colleagues to take risks, the company was finally able to manufacture a "film strip" of Listerine into a soluble material that would have the desired effect, fit in a pocket or purse, and achieve profitable results.

To achieve these remarkable accomplishments, they infused a set of creative conditions that stimulated abundant possibilities and passion at all levels in the company. "Weave innovation into everything we do" became an enduring mantra and legacy for Pfizer Consumer Healthcare's CEO Marc Robinson, who coined the phrase. It became a passionate rallying cry for each of 3,500 employees to think big and build a culture of rapid and profound innovation.

This tingly breath freshener was one of the first and most profound designs to emerge as a result of weaving innovative conditions. However, Robinson and his team were not satisfied with just one breakthrough innovation; they were interested in cultivating growth to become the

NOTHING GREAT IN THE WORLD HAS BEEN ACCOMPLISHED WITHOUT PASSION.

—Christian Friedrich Hebbel,
German poet

number-one health-care company. Listerine Pocket Paks was a key first spark, and it helped produce a stimulating effect that ignited a passion for more innovation. It also encouraged a can-do mind-set that helped set the tone for further innovation. It did not happen all at once, and in some cases the change occurred slowly, but because of committed leadership and passionate intention around creative/innovative outcomes and aesthetic qualities of change, they were able to produce many sparks of innovation and consequently many business results. The senior team put a new product development process in place, developed new metrics of success to encourage more risk taking, trained an extensive number of "green and black belt" leaders to improve their ideation and prototyping techniques, came up with new rewards to help align innovation-related goals, and devised sophisticated communication systems that helped keep colleagues informed about innovation-related achievements. They also created many stimulating spaces, such as an aesthetically pleasing area with comfy couches and one area with floor-to-ceiling whiteboards. These spaces encouraged dialogue and helped to ingrain innovation into the organization's culture.

Practical and convenient health solutions and remedies were the benefits consumers reaped from these creative conditions. To the colleagues who wove these creative patterns of behavior, their success was a reflection of their many sparks, inner passions, and desire to win through innovation.

Oh, the Places (and Spaces) We Can Go!

The last book Dr. Seuss wrote and illustrated, *Oh, the Places You'll Go!* is a story about a young boy simply referred to as "you." "You" discovers he has the brains and feet to choose any direction he would like to take in life. The process of cultivating your creative genius works in a similar fashion. During his journey, "you" goes to many places, some "wide open," some "waiting," and some that have unexpected twists and turns and ups and downs. This sounds like life described in a nutshell, doesn't it? We have many spaces and places to choose from that could stimulate a creative spark and unlock our creative genius.

In the world of Seuss, "Things can happen" and "frequently do" to people who are as "brainy and footsy" as "you." This is a wonderful way of describing how the process of cultivating our creative genius is a conscious choice and how there may be unintended—and hopefully pleasurable—consequences that inspire us to cultivate even more sparks. If you pay attention to what stimulates you and remain focused on your creative outcomes and the aesthetics that best suit your creative challenge, then you can produce conditions that are ripe for stimulated action. While you cannot always anticipate what specific ideas will come to you, we are sure that the more you cultivate the right set of conditions, the more likely you will be to have spark moments.

Between 1901 and 1902 the famous composer Gustav Mahler composed Symphony No. 5, which many claim to be his best symphony, at his summer cottage near a lake in Austria. Having earned the reputation of being a "vacation composer," Mahler had spent many summers with his family at the Inn Foettinger in Steinbach, Austria. While the inn was ideal for a vacation retreat, it was not an ideal place for Mahler to work because the other guests of the inn often disturbed his concentration. As a result, he had a cottage built on the edge of the lake near the inn to provide him a quiet space to listen to the music in his head. The peace of this cottage, supplemented by regular walks in the meadow, provided him with the appropriate stimulation to perfect his compositions. For us, just as it was for Mahler, the key to attracting more spark moments is to pick the right places and create the right spaces. You may be in a place where you are away from mundane distractions; however, if you do not have the right "space," it will still be hard for you to perpetuate creative thought and action compatible to your objectives. Be conscious of both.

So what is the right environment for you to be creative or tackle a challenge that requires a creative solution? What are the catalysts you can leverage to inspire you? Where are the spaces and places that help focus your creativity? Where are the ones that unleash it? Where do you go to

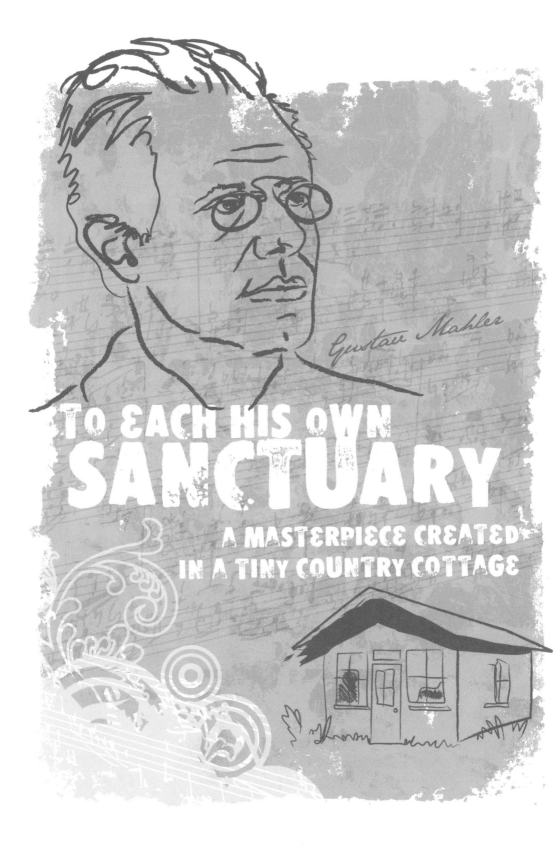

Gustav Mahler

TO EACH HIS OWN
SANCTUARY

A MASTERPIECE CREATED
IN A TINY COUNTRY COTTAGE

generate your best ideas? As we described in the chapter on scouting, some people go outside their homes or offices to generate a more stimulating environment. Edison, for example, liked to fish to help calm himself, and Thoreau took long walks near Walden Pond or holed up in his cabin to inspire his poetry. Others, however, are most comfortable only in an environment that they consider their own.

A STRONG PASSION FOR ANY OBJECT WILL ENSURE SUCCESS, FOR THE DESIRE OF THE END WILL POINT OUT THE MEANS.

—WILLIAM HAZLITT, BRITISH AUTHOR

To optimize your creative spark potential, you must first become aware of the environmental stimuli that work best for you. If you need inspiration, maybe listening to soft classical music will get your creative juices flowing. Or maybe you need the energy level that rock-and-roll can provide.

Setting is also important. Maybe you prefer to be near water, or maybe a dense forest. Maybe all you need is a picture of a beautiful ocean to free your mind and let it drift into a blissful state of creativity. Or maybe a warm cup of tea and a well-worn leather chair will help you concentrate. You have many fertile spaces and places to nurture your creative genius. When you are motivated to cultivate these spaces and places, the sparks are unlimited.

TIPS FOR CULTIVATING

- Differentiate and experiment with personal, pack, and public workspaces. Personal: quiet time alone; Pack: small-group conversation; and Public: gathering as a larger community.
- Discover what types of sounds stimulate you the most.
- Experiment with different sitting and writing surfaces to find the one you prefer.
- Chose the level of light you like best. Do you prefer natural lighting or dim, candlelit settings?
- Think about a creative challenge and draw or write a description of the spaces and places that will inspire you the most in answering it.
- Clear your desk.
- Post some quotes up on your wall.
- Visit many different environments—a park, a café, a library, a theater, a museum—and observe how each makes you feel. Journal what it is about each of these places that makes you feel as you do.
- Rearrange your furniture and add color to your workspace.
- Add artwork, plants, and artifacts to provide inspiration.
- Give Saori a try and see what you produce!

CULTIVATE
THE FERTILE
SPACES AND PLACES
THAT NURTURE
YOUR CREATIVE
GENIUS

BOLD
EXPERIMENTAL
JOYFUL
CURIOUS
Yippee!
DREAMER
ENTHUSIASTIC
CONFIDENT
IN THE MOMENT
PLAYING

CHAPTER 5

Amuse Yourself:
Playing with Possibilities

Just eighteen miles away from the hustle and bustle of Manhattan sits the epicenter of our creative expression, emerging from the banks of the mighty Hudson River. Perched atop a hill, our office and our home are surrounded by trees, stone, and undulating hills. Often we awake to beaming sunshine, stunning views, and the dawn of new possibilities.

Because of our beautiful natural surroundings and proximity to a large city, we are able to entertain ourselves in myriad parks, squares, piers, coffee houses, museums, and restaurants. In the ebb and flow of the river and the migrating geese and the sweet sculptural sounds of music buzzing in the nightclubs and great restaurants, we have an amazing playground before us that stimulates our senses and invites us to create and live fully each day.

But you don't have to live in an Eden or a thriving metropolis to spark creative moments. You do not have to have a particularly exotic sandbox in which to amuse yourself. All you need is a fertile imagination and a willingness to play. When we strum the strings on a guitar or throw a ball or join in on an icebreaker activity before a business meeting, we are choosing to play and open ourselves up to possibilities.

> # THE CREATION
> ## OF SOMETHING NEW IS NOT ACCOMPLISHED
> # BY THE INTELLECT
> ### BUT BY THE PLAY INSTINCT
> ### ACTING FROM INNER NECESSITY.
> ## THE CREATIVE MIND PLAYS
> ## WITH OBJECTS IT LOVES.
>
> —CARL JUNG, SWISS PSYCHIATRIST

Within our daily lives we are constantly (and usually unconsciously) provided with opportunities to play and amuse ourselves with possibilities. No matter whether you are in your car driving to work or you are attending a mundane social event, an invitation to play and be creative awaits you. Every day is a reminder to awaken our creative genius. Every day offers a gift of play. So long as we are willing to jump in and become present in opening up and examining the contents of this gift, we will know that a surprise awaits us. The more we integrate play into our daily lives, the more we will increase our chances for creative success and put ourselves in a relaxed state where all things seem possible. So why not just jump in and play?

Play, Stimulation, and Creativity

The results of applying your creativity to generate a big idea can be very serious. However, the process you use doesn't need to be. You can still get results if you inject play into the process to spark creative ideas and action.

Jesse Posa, an actor and Frank Sinatra impersonator, is the consummate player when it comes to lifting the spirits and energy of others. Full of great energy, passion, and mirth, Jesse views his world as a stage on which to perform and entertain. Whether you are at the golf links or having an important conversation about his business, he finds a way to entertain you and make the best use of his surroundings. Every moment you spend with Jesse is an invitation to have fun, think big, and let your imagination run free. "When I conduct a performance," Posa says, "there's got to be juices flowing to help me stimulate and infuse others with energy. It's a give-and-take with the audience—I feed off their energy, they feed off mine. When they are demonstrative or appreciative of what I am doing, then I am stimulated. I may not always get that from the full audience so I deliberately play to those who I can engage in most and strive to make a connection that eventually pleases the entire audience." Jesse's way of being is playfulness, and the lens through which he views the world is oriented toward possibilities.

You are like a human transmission tower, transmitting a frequency with your thoughts. If you want to change anything in your life, change the frequency by changing your thoughts.

—RHONDA BYRNE, AUTHOR OF *The Secret*

When we are in play mode we entertain and express ourselves. We bring energy into the room and create ripe conditions where literally anything is possible and anything might happen. Spontaneity and serendipity are abundant when we are in a playful state of mind—it begins in our thoughts and follows through in our feelings and, consequently, our actions. When we play, we are free from constraint. Many people we've spoken to in our workshops say that when they play and act more playfully they are most like themselves. "When I perform and play before an audience," says Posa, "I bring my full self into public view and feel authentic."

YOU CAN **LEARN MORE** ABOUT A PERSON IN AN HOUR OF PLAY THAN IN A YEAR OF **CONVERSATION.**

—PLATO, CLASSICAL GREEK PHILOSOPHER

Though Einstein is most often associated with big, important, heady ideas and formulas, he had a reputation for being a practical joker, having fun, and engaging in some type of physical activity daily, such as riding a bike, in order to spark his imagination. Engaging in playful activity helps geniuses like Einstein get charged up (No wonder his hair looked like it did!) and prepared to create. After many years of teaching others to work together more collaboratively, solve problems, and be more innovative, we have found that injecting play will not only create more fun, but it will also stimulate and ready the senses for creative action.

Play is serious business. We believe that when people have a chance to unwind and let loose, their natural endorphins kick in and put them in the proper physical and mental state to think and act creatively. We often start off our seminars with some playful activity that simply loosens people up both physically and mentally in order to get them engaged and focused on the here and now. Creative genius must have a steady diet of fun, expression, and imaginative spirit.

Just think back to the times when you've seen a speaker use relevant humor (play) to begin her presentation. How did that make you feel? Assuming it was actually funny and relevant, chances are you laughed and felt relaxed and more engaged. A playful speaker can connect with her audience and give them permission to be playful and open to spark moments as well as herself. When the audience is in this state of engagement and play, they are more open to learning, more open to ideas, more open to possibilities, and more open to spark moments. So the next time you are giving a presentation, think about how you might incorporate some play into it.

IMAGINATION VS. KNOWLEDGE

Imagination: ability and process to invent personal realms within the mind from elements derived from sense perceptions of the shared world; free from constraints

Knowledge: facts, information, and skills acquired through experience or education; the psychological result of perception, learning, and reasoning

What Is Play?

The difficulty of embracing play as a stimulant and fostering it as a habit stems from the fact that we have too narrowly defined the word "play." When it comes to organizations, especially, few people would consider themselves playful or value play as a legitimate way to spur business results. But play doesn't have to be streamers and balloons; play may be as simple as getting someone to laugh or acting out a process that on paper is hard to conceptualize.

Play has always been an important way for humans to express ourselves, unwind, and create. Since the beginning, we have used some form of play to act out our stories, experiences, and rituals. From art on caves to the epic Olympic games of Greece, play is part of who we are and how we like to express ourselves. And from an evolutionary standpoint, research shows that if we frequently play, our cerebellum (also referred to as the "little brain," a region of the brain that plays an important role in the integration

of sensory perception and motor output) will increase in size. Whether we pursue it through dance, theater, sport, or using Koosh balls in a meeting, play is an essential part of human nature and can help us to conceptualize, experiment, manipulate, and build something more effectively.

At one point in the 1800s, psychologists declared that play was driven by surplus energy and was nothing more than aimless expenditure of energy that would need to be managed in order to live a disciplined and productive life. Yikes! No wonder many still have the attitude that play is surplus and something reserved exclusively for off-time and recreational activity. Of course, we couldn't disagree more!

Play is a form of recreation that spurs a feeling of freshness or something new. The word "creation" means to produce, engender, or cause something. The Latin origin of the word "create" is *creare*, which means to grow. Recreation, then, is a process of perpetually growing or reinventing ourselves in order to produce that new, fresh perspective. The more we recreate, the more we grow. The more we grow, the more we renew and bring freshness to our everyday existence. Therefore, play is a recreation activity that helps us to both grow and stay fresh. Play is a refreshing way to stimulate our energy and enliven our creative sprits in order to grow and produce new things. It is spontaneous and unconventional. So why wouldn't organizations and the people in them be interested in creating something that is new and that brings freshness, with the added benefits of more creative and relaxed states of mind? Is that not what innovation is all about—creating something that is new and fresh?

A man who completely exemplifies and embodies playfulness and living a recreation-filled life is Larry Barker. Throughout his life, Larry has played many varied roles. He received his PhD at twenty-three; became a full professor at twenty-nine; has written numerous articles, business books, and college textbooks; and has always kept himself active and stimulated through his playful spirit. Says Larry, "Early on in life I identified with the college professor, but at twenty-nine I had a eureka moment that there was more to life than just being a professor. I needed games to play to give me purpose, some fun new ways to approach the old and develop other skills, so I found new games to play. Music was always my primary game and I was able to bring that into the classroom." He needed recreation, and he was able to bring his expression, his play, into the work that he did as a college professor. And, by the way, just because he had this eureka moment that there was more to life than being a college professor, don't think for a moment that he was disengaged and ineffective. In fact, it was just the opposite: his realization was exactly *why* he was effective. He was a brilliant professor, mentor, and example to his students of what it meant to be fully engaged in life and to love what you do and go after it—playfully. These days you can find Larry mentoring others in business and life, writing and performing music, fishing, playing (and winning!) blackjack tournaments around the country, and writing books covering many business and human-interest topics—even meditation!

THE MOST POTENT MUSE OF ALL IS OUR INNER CHILD.

—STEPHEN NACHMANOVITCH,
AMERICAN MUSICIAN AND EDUCATOR

Letting Go

To be creative, you must play. To spark and activate your creative side, you must be willing to summon a childlike self with a fearless and unrestricted attitude that allows you to take risks, have fun, zig and zag in the moment, and exercise your imaginative spirit. The more we consciously engage in some sort of play, the more likely we are to spark creative moments and generate positive reactions in others. As a way of letting your hair down— or "up" in the case of Einstein—play is a natural forum for expressing yourself, making yourself vulnerable, and ultimately boosting your confidence in your own ideas and the ways in which you feel comfortable communicating with others.

....

DID YoU KNoW ...

Did you know that a typical kindergarten student laughs three hundred times a day, but the average adult laughs just seventeen times a day?

(From William Fry, professor of psychiatry at Stanford University Medical School)

....

However, many of us are inhibited in play because of what seems like a widespread aversion to letting ourselves go and simply having fun. We often hear people say things like "I don't want to make a fool of myself" or "No one will take me seriously if I start to play or be playful." It is when we say the word "serious" that things often go awry. It suggests that play cannot convey or express something of importance or substance. We have lost count now of the many executive boardrooms we have walked into where it was clear they were just not interested in having much fun. On many occasions the senior team members were so stiff that the portraits of bygone leaders plastered to the wall had more life in them than they did. Many teams would rather remain silent, expressionless, and phlegmatic than become enthusiastic and playful.

Often when we are called in to help build a more creative and innovative organization the leaders express a desire to generate more ideas, improve the mobility and quality of ideas, and, in general, build a more lively and energetic organization. However, the moment we begin to engage a client, it's not unusual to experience resistance to play as a way to stimulate creative ideas and action. You can almost see the bubbles popping above their heads, saying things like "Oh, no! Here comes a bunch of touchy-feely types," or "Innovation is important, but I hope we don't have to do any of those silly creativity exercises." The typical business professional and leader prefers serious, chart-filled, numbers-oriented, case study–rich PowerPoint presentations instead as the way to stimulate creativity and spark big ideas.

CREATIVITY REQUIRES THE COURAGE TO LET GO OF CERTAINTIES.

—ERICH FROMM, GERMAN PSYCHOLOGIST, PSYCHOANALYST, PHILOSOPHER

A couple of years back, we were leading a group of soon-to-be black-belt innovators (a level of innovation certification that denotes expertise in skills to help others innovate, lead innovation initiative teams, etc.) for a consumer goods company. Included in this group were two very senior team members, one from marketing and the other from research and development. The team was tasked with understanding the "healthy habits" of people from the ages of eighteen to twenty-two. We encouraged them to obtain novel and "edgy" insights into how young people take care of their bodies. Inspired by this assignment, these two senior-level innovators ventured into the heart of New York City, eventually winding up at a tattoo parlor. They spent some time interviewing the manager of the store, as well as some of the patrons within the age-group parameters. Not only did they gain many valuable insights about skin care, they also had fun learning about a subject they knew nothing about. To commemorate their experience, they each got temporary tattoos on their shoulders. When they returned from their experience with their tattoos, not only did their colleagues share a good laugh, but their playful action inspired others to let loose as well. From that point on the other team members relaxed and took more risks. This was especially remarkable because the organization was known to be very conservative and risk averse. "It completely

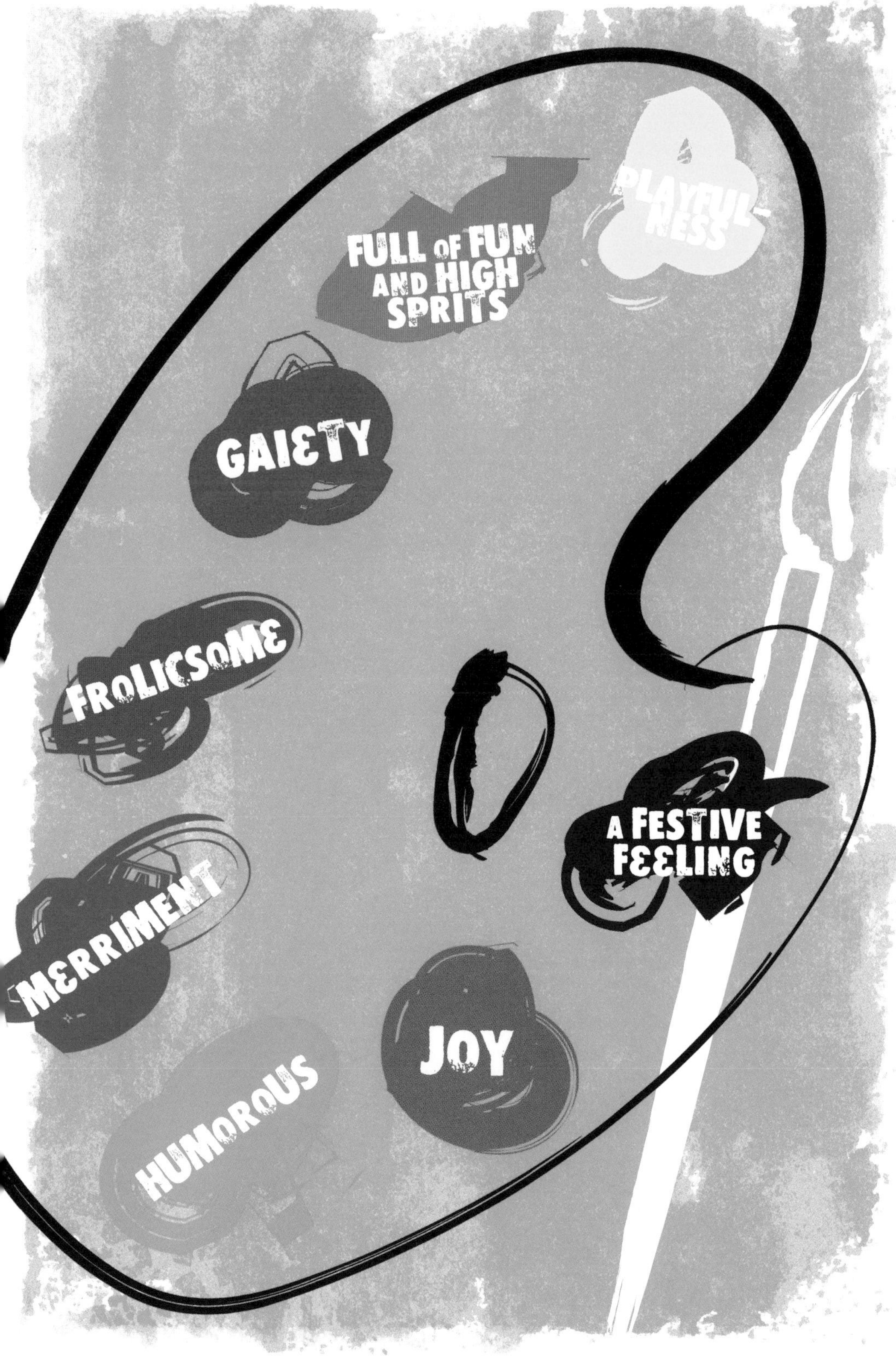
PLAYFUL-NESS
FULL OF FUN AND HIGH SPRITS
GAIETY
FROLICSOME
A FESTIVE FEELING
MERRIMENT
JOY
HUMOROUS

puts you at ease when you just go out and play," said one of the tattooed leaders, "and it makes mixing fun with work no longer a taboo."

PLAY: THE ELIXIR OF CREATIVITY

Take a sheet of paper and write, draw, or free-associate words in response to each of these questions.

- When you were growing up, what kind of play activity brought you the most pleasure?
- When you were playing, what kind of objects, instruments, or materials did you use?
- Did you like building things? Or did you like taking things apart?
- Do you doodle or draw?
- Do you have at least one belly laugh a day?
- What were your favorite games while growing up?
- Did you spend time daydreaming?
- Do you daydream now?
- What do you do every day to stay refreshed?
- If you were to create a game, what would it be?

To foster genuine play, open-mindedness is necessary to help us move beyond our inhibitions and balance the occasions when "serious" or more reserved expression is considered more appropriate. Chances are, you are already playful. However, you may not fully and consciously integrate and cultivate your playful side as a way to stimulate your creative genius. As we said before, every day you have the opportunity to play to prepare you for the day or to balance personal and work priorities. Whatever way you decide to use it, play can help you to manage things more effectively and expand your "playing field."

Imaginative Play:
Indulging Your Dreams and Fantasies

Any object can serve multiple purposes no matter what it has been origi-
nally designed and classified for. General uses for a ball, for example, may
include throwing it, rolling it, or hitting it. However, a ball can also represent a planet among a galaxy of other planets. It may serve as a doorstop
or a cushion (depending on how large the ball is in relationship to your
bottom). How we view and use a simple toy such as a ball is left only to
our imagination.

Children are especially adept at using their imagination, especially
when playing. Think back on your childhood, to how fun it was to make
up stories in the dark with your friends and let your imagination run wild
within the safe confines of your blanket tent, where your flashlight was
your sole source of illumination. From one story after another all you had
to rely on was your own imagination and the imagination of others as you
built upon the collective energy of the group. Sometimes scary, sometimes
silly, the stories you made up kept you and your friends excited and stimulated. Inside the tent, together with your friends, you were liberated from
distraction and free to imagine a universe of possibilities. Perhaps this is
why dreams are so unfettered by any rules or boundaries, because our
mind unconsciously blocks out the realities exposed in the light of day.

Shelly Walsh of Tabi International uses a variety of media to stimulate
a playful environment. She is known for bringing in a lot of props from
her travels around the world. As Shelly travels, she is always collecting and
picking up things she thinks might stimulate an idea. One season she and
her team designed a line of fashion that represented a Heritage Christmas
theme. When we asked her how she came up with the concepts for the
design, she immediately stood up from behind her desk and walked us
into their design room.

The first thing we noticed was a huge white table covered with fabrics,
clippings from magazines, and various artifacts she had collected in her

travels. She showed us the images she had collected one by one and immediately had us imagining that we were in England in the 1800s, walking down a cobbled street, the clip-clopping of horses' hooves in the distance. "When I am in the process of developing a new design concept," says Walsh, "I start to buy a lot of different objects and use them as props to play with concepts and stimulate ideas relevant to our brand and our design objectives." She described the process of discovering each object in vivid detail: buying Christmas lights that sparkle brightly to mark the opening of the holiday season, strapping on a pair of well-worn boots to contend with a winter's snow, putting on a tartan scarf to insulate the neck from the cold, getting out ornate tins to wrap and preserve a set of freshly baked cookies, and so forth and so on. As she described each prop and how she used it, we were swept away by her stories of exotic travels. Her descriptions of each scene had the same feel as a child's fantasy play or show-and-tell experience. With classical music playing softly in the background, Walsh pulled us deeper and deeper into her imagination. She held our attention and connected with us. She was playing to our senses of touch, smell, and feel. She helped us, through the use of props and storytelling, visualize the theme Tabi International was planning to build into the design of a new line of clothing. We were entranced. "I start simple," she said, "and then we have a conversation about the topic. I bring in more props, we play with the concepts, and then morph them into a story that we will eventually weave into our brand strategy, designs, and selection of seasonal apparel."

Our exchange with Shelly Walsh helped us feel more engaged than if we were just having a casual conversation or listening passively to her walk through a deck of PowerPoint slides. Within a very short period of time the power of a simple "show and tell" played beautifully to our imagination.

LETTING YOUR MIND PLAY IS THE BEST WAY TO SOLVE PROBLEMS.

—BILL WATTERMAN, CREATOR OF "CALVIN AND HOBBES"

HOLD FAST TO DREAMS
FOR IF DREAMS DIE
LIFE IS A BROKEN-WINGED BIRD
THAT CANNOT FLY.
HOLD FAST TO DREAMS
FOR WHEN DREAMS GO
LIFE IS A BARREN FIELD
FROZEN WITH SNOW.

—"Dreams" BY LANGSTON HUGHES,
AMERICAN POET AND PLAYWRIGHT

When you engage in imaginative play you have an opportunity to liberate your senses and explore who you are through the fantasy of the moment and the objects or circumstances that permit you to exercise your creative mind. So, as you consider taking on your next challenge, or if you feel like you are stuck in a rut like our friend David from Dublin, think back to your childhood days and indulge yourself with some imaginative play.

> *There is nothing like a dream to create the future.*
> —Victor Hugo, French poet and novelist

DID YOU KNOW . . .

Did you know that psychologists estimate that one-third to one-half of a person's thoughts while awake are daydreams?

"Our creativity naturally flourishes in childhood," writes Sandra Magsamen in her book *Living Artfully*, "but at some point, we are all confronted with grown-up rules." These rules become ever more constraining as time passes, and, consequently, we lose the ability to spark creative moments and utilize our creative brains. The beauty of a child's imaginative play is that there are no rules. To expand your creative playing field, it is imperative to imagine possibilities and play along with your dreams and fantasies from time to time, because you never know where they may lead you.

Don't dis daydreaming! From this day forth, give yourself permission to daydream! According to WebMD, daydreaming can be beneficial in many ways and can even boost productivity. Daydreams help you to

- Relax
- Manage conflict

- Maintain relationships
- Cement your beliefs and values
- Boost creativity and achieve goals
- Relieve boredom

So next time you find yourself needing a boost or new perspective, let your (day)dreams come alive!

> *What happens if we let our dream world constructively intersect with our waking life? What if we pay creative attention to our dreams, consciously allowing their imagery, patterns, and forms into our waking consciousness?*
>
> —JILL MELLICK, AUTHOR OF *The Art of Dreaming*

Physical Play: It's Time to Limber Up and Turn Up the Heat!

We live in a climate where the winters can be quite harsh and the temperatures frigid. To make matters worse, we live in a home that boasts great views of the Hudson River—but is severely inadequate when it comes to insulation. Brrrr. Consequently, one of our favorite sports is competing for our dog's attention because of her natural warmth and ability to serve as a portable electric blanket. In addition to our four-legged warmer and generous amounts of hot tea, the best way we have to stay warm is through exercise. Exercise is not only a perfect way to elevate our body temperatures, but it also is a great way to limber us up for our day, which often demands a lot of stand-up presentation and facilitation. Being physical gets us in a fluid and relaxed state to create and help others create.

Our bodies are important instruments of communication and creation. How we use them holds enormous potential for not only how we maintain our energy, but also our capacity to manipulate and build things. We feel the success of how we communicate and create is largely determined by how we engage in physical play or other restorative activity to keep us limber and flexible. And research has confirmed the critical link between physical activity and stimulation of the creative mind. The more we use our bodies and engage them in our daily activities, the more likely we will have the energy and heat to spark our creative genius.

Physical energy is the fundamental source of fuel . . . it not only lies at the heart of alertness and vitality but also affects our ability to manage our emotions, sustain concentration, think creatively, and even maintain our commitment to whatever mission we are on.

—JIM LOEHR AND TONY SCHWARTZ, AUTHORS OF
The Power of Full Engagement

Physical play includes conventional kinds of physical activity, such as exercising at a gym, playing sports, or simply stretching, but it also includes such things as drawing, cutting, model building, and other con-structive activities that allow us to move our muscles and flex our minds. Even simple breathing exercises or related movement activity increases the likelihood that we will be more aware of stimuli and thus more oppor-tunities in which to express ourselves.

Marc Newberg of HON, whom we spoke about in chapter 3, is a health and fitness nut. He usually exercises forty-five to sixty minutes a day, and when his travel schedule demands are particularly hectic, he finds creative and simple ways to move his body to give him what he refers to as a "clean and refreshed" feeling. In addition to staying fit, New-berg explains that having "some form of physical activity stimulates a thermal state for me that puts me in a proper state of mind to tackle the demands of my job and in general my life. In addition, it's fun for me to exercise because during the time in which I am exercising my body I am also exercising my mind to work through problems and in some instances develop big ideas."

....

DID YOU KNOW . . .

Did you know that 40 percent of America's household pets are over-weight and that 78 percent of Americans don't meet basic activity-level recommendations?

....

Improvisational Play: Go with the Flow

Improvisation is an activity that many musicians link to jazz. However, long before jazz arrived on the music scene, improvisation was integral to classical music—up until the early 1900s, when it was no longer hip to riff, so to speak. Enter Franz (Ferenc) Liszt, the famous Hungarian composer. No classical composer corroborated the idea that improvisa-tion was essential to help develop skill, stamina, and creative expression in classical music more than Liszt. Known for his complex and involved pieces, such as the "Hungarian Rhapsody," this composer, first taught by his father and a virtuoso at age twelve, was also considered to be a flashy performer and a master at improvisation. He was reputed to have been able to hear an opera one day and incorporate elements of the opera's composition into his concert the very next day. Liszt is also credited for having invented the modern piano recital. He often performed fully improvised concerts as a way to express his ideas with creativity and originality. What a show-off, huh?

Well, you don't necessarily have to be a master composer like Liszt to be effective at improvisational play and have some fun. Improvisa-tional play is a habit of behaving, creating, and being completely in touch, playfully speaking with the stimuli around you. From a psychological perspective, improvisation helps promote greater self-awareness and understanding of the actions you perform. Improvisational play promotes spontaneity, flexibility, and the motivation to try new things. When you

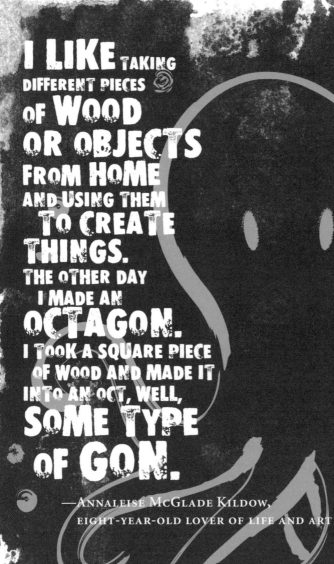

I LIKE TAKING DIFFERENT PIECES OF WOOD OR OBJECTS FROM HOME AND USING THEM TO CREATE THINGS. THE OTHER DAY I MADE AN OCTAGON. I TOOK A SQUARE PIECE OF WOOD AND MADE IT INTO AN OCT, WELL, SOME TYPE OF GON.

—ANNALEISE McGLADE KILDOW,
EIGHT-YEAR-OLD LOVER OF LIFE AND ART

act and react in response to stimuli, spark moments are inevitable. The quality and quantity of your creative spark moments will depend on how open you are to trying new behaviors and engaging in new possibilities. New possibilities can result from improvisational play with the creation of new ideas, models, insights, structures, and symbols—or, as in the case of Liszt, compositions. By stimulating your imagination and bringing your personal awareness more into the moment, improvisational play increases the likelihood that you will attract spark moments and consequently activate your creative genius.

However, as with other forms of play, not everyone is comfortable with improv because it involves a certain amount of risk and vulnerability. The idea of being onstage is frightening to most. Many of us would prefer to be spectators rather than active participants. Developing an atmosphere of trust that allows people the freedom to take chances and build upon the spontaneity of others is key to making improvisation an acceptable habit and effective practice for generating creative ideas. We will talk more about cultivating and the importance of building trust in stimulating creative results later, but for now the important point is that the success of improvisational play hinges upon successful social acceptance and interaction. In other words, the better those arround you support improvisation, the more this form of creative expression will work for you.

So, what do we mean by improvisational play, and why is this a helpful habit for sparking your creative genius? Improvisational play generally follows some combination of the following three simple principles: play on the fly, play to have fun, and play that encourages others to play along with you.

Playing on the fly helps you to fuse the situation and tools you have available at the time and select the options that fit best to achieve your desired effect. When we watched Robin Williams on *Inside the Actors Studio*, he went up to a woman in the audience and asked to borrow her scarf. Within seconds he had the audience laughing uproariously at the many different impersonations he was creating in real time, from an Indian woman wearing a sari to someone wearing a skirt. He used a simple object to make a connection with the audience, and profoundly demonstrated that it doesn't take much to begin sparking your creative senses. It's fun to assume different roles and play out different scenarios. It helps you and others achieve a relaxed state of mind, which is fundamental to the creative process.

IMPROMPTU IMPROV

We often play this game with our daughter as part of her bedtime routine. And we must give her the credit, because she taught us the game. We promise you don't need to be the next Robin Williams, and you don't even need to act this out (though extra credit goes to those of you who do!), but here's a chance to put your secret improv skills into action. Here's how it works.

Start with the statement below and create a story with a beginning, middle, and end that includes a lesson for life. "**I was walking down the street on a cold rainy day when I stumbled upon . . .**" As you tell the story, work to incorporate the following elements/phrases into the story:

- Children playing on their bikes
- A garbage can overflowing with trash
- A car accident
- Spaghetti
- Creativity
- Philosophy
- Three little pigs
- Paper

Have fun with this. Use the list we've provided or make up your own. Try different starting phrases. There are no right or wrong ways of playing.

A simple way to illustrate how improvisational play can be powerful and fun is through shared storytelling, meaning one person begins the story however he or she would like, and then everyone takes turns adding to the story, until they reach a logical and intuitive ending. The shared storytelling structure provides a focus and a framework that allows people not only to express themselves, but also to have meaningful creative exchange. The point of this improvisational activity is not how good people are at telling a story, but to see if something fun, something coherent results despite the fact that no one person is controlling the story.

Improvisational play encourages esprit de corps, connection, and collaboration between people and groups. Encouraging others to create something out of nothing is just another form of brainstorming new ideas.

**IMAGINATION IS EVERYTHING.
IT IS THE PREVIEW
OF LIFE'S COMING ATTRACTIONS.**
—Albert Einstein, German physicist

Finding Your Playful Muse

To play is to amuse—ourselves and others. The word "amuse" derives from the Latin word *muse,* which comes from the Greek word *mousa. Mousa* means to think and to meditate on a subject. Finding your playful muse is all about tapping into your playful self, attracting spark moments, and being inspired. When you muse about something—whether it's a song, an idea, or a concept—you are using your imagination to transform the world of reality into a world of unlimited possibility. What if I could fly? What if I could travel the world? What if I could be and do anything that I desire? Give yourself permission to find your playful muse and spend some time getting to know her.

When we muse we give ourselves a chance to try on new roles, shape new paths, and have abundant fun along the way. When we assume many different characters, utilize many different props, and get stimulated, we not only promote a greater level of understanding of ourselves, but also form stronger connections to others by modeling playful behavior and encouraging them to pursue their own creative impulses. In preparation for a performance, Jesse Posa becomes the method actor and immerses himself completely in his character. He says, "I start being in character when I put on my costume, place a cigarette in one hand and a drink in another, slug a trenchcoat over my shoulder, and put on a hat. From that point on, I *am* Frank Sinatra, ready to transform my audience." He becomes his muse. He is transformed, and his creative action begins to flow.

Whether we are singing or reciting poetry or using props or building sand castles, when we play, anything is possible. The more we leverage play, the more we expand our field of creativity.

I remember now how children love to play. I look around and see math and science things disguised as wire, wood and foam, bamboo, colored plastic rings, colored tubes, fabric, yarn, and many other things. Let me get my hands on them so I can play and learn and remember the child inside me.

—WALTER F. DREW, EARLY-CHILDHOOD EDUCATOR

TIPS FOR PLAYING

- Try something new—a new game, a new approach, a new food.
- Be willing to get your hands dirty—literally. Go outside and dig, build, play in sand if there's a beach nearby. Make a sand castle, design it with seashells, and pretend that you are entering a sand castle contest for the best design.
- Have a playful attitude. Don't take yourself or others too seriously.
- Watch a funny movie.
- If you have kids of your own (or if you can borrow some from a friend), watch them play, take note, and try it yourself.
- Get physical. Exercising your body will exercise your mind!
- Let yourself get lost in your daydreams.
- Journal about those daydreams. What are they telling you, how might you learn from what catches your attention when you daydream?
- How about those nighttime dreams? Start a dream journal and see what your dreams are telling you about your creative genius.
- Put together that scrapbook you never have the time to get to.
- Remember how you played as a child—what were your favorite things to do? Why? Think about how you might incorporate some of the lessons from your childhood into what you do today.
- Do a crossword puzzle, take an art class, dust off your guitar and play!
- Dance in your living room (or office!) with some stimulating music.
- Take Fido for a walk!
- Think of at least one hundred uses for a chair. Right now, do it!
- Write a poem about your life, your goals, or the person you love.
- Meditate. Clear your mind of the clutter to allow space for the fun stuff.
- Call the friend who always makes you laugh.

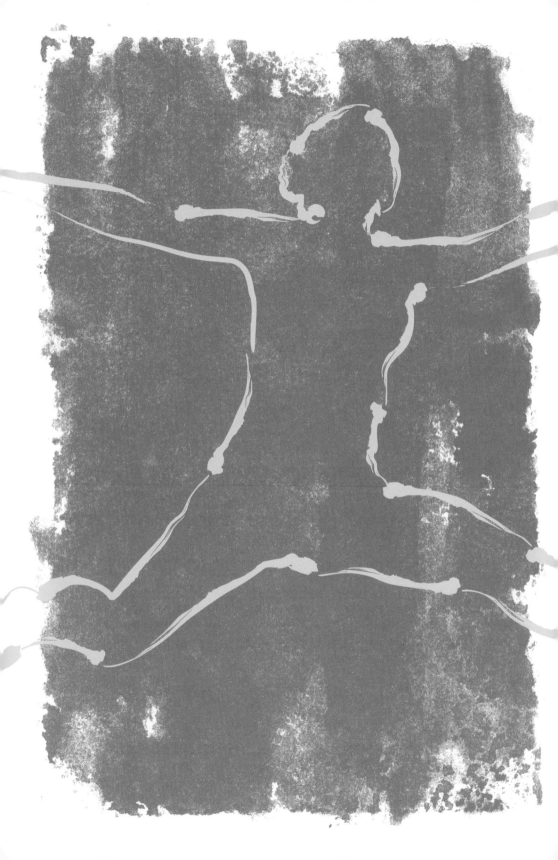

Chapter 6

Make the Leap:
Venturing into the Unknown

When we are not traveling or rushing off to a client meeting, we usually awaken very early to the whimpering of our beautiful and energetic Hungarian Viszla, Sienna. Every morning, like clockwork, she sounds off to signal that she is ready to begin her day, and her incessant cries coax us to rise up and take her on a brisk run or walk.

We take Sienna to an area that, in the wee hours of the morning, looks more like a dark and mysterious forest from some Tolkienesque fantasy than a friendly and inviting suburban park. As you approach the path, it's easy to get a little spooked by the swaying trees and the bristling grass. Aside from an occasional chirp from a songbird or squawk from the geese, the morning hours are eerily silent. But nothing seems to stop Sienna from venturing further into the woods. Apart from an occasional glance back in search of a treat, she lunges forward undaunted as if in search of prey. She is not focused on any end point, concerned only with pursuing the smells and sounds that are stimulating her senses. A natural field dog with an uncanny instinct for finding birds and other furry animals, she pulls us deeper and deeper into the park. If not for her fearlessness, we're not sure we would be courageous enough to head down the dimly lit paths.

ONLY WITH **ABSOLUTE**
FEARLESSNESS
CAN WE SLAY THE DRAGONS
OF **MEDIOCRITY**
THAT INVADE OUR GARDENS.

—GEORGE LOIS, LEGENDARY
ADVERTISING COMMUNICATOR

It's easy to understand and appreciate the zeal with which our little pup pursues a path without much, if any, contemplation. After all, dogs act purely on instinct. They are obedient to what drives them naturally: food, water, play, protection, and survival. At that same basic level, humans are no different. We are bundles of survival instincts that help us to keep alive and ward off threatening circumstances or people. However, unlike our fine four-footed friends, we are sophisticated, thinking beings that can consciously choose different and creative paths based on our remarkable reasoning abilities. But sometimes our reasoning abilities keep us from those creative paths rather than driving us on to them. Sometimes we attach ourselves to a spark of inspiration, and sometimes we ignore it altogether. But being stimulated means keeping our creative sparks at the forefront of our journey and appreciating that there may be real or perceived risks when we pursue our creative paths. Venturing down the paths of our creative impulses and sparks, especially in our work world, is a particularly delicate process at times and thus requires a great deal of faith in ourselves and passion for our pursuits.

RISK TAKER
COURAGEOUS
ADVERTURESOME
PATHFINDER
AUTHENTIC
HONEST
CONFIDENT
COMMITTED
VENTURING!

FOLLOW YOUR INSTINCTS. THAT'S WHERE TRUE WISDOM MANIFESTS ITSELF.

—OPRAH WINFREY, MEDIA ENTREPRENEUR

Taking the Unknown Path

In the business world, we expect things to be clear, exact, and predictable. Corporations value the tried and true, the effective, efficient, and known paths of success. In contrast, when we choose a path of creativity, we naturally lean toward possibilities, expressions, and ideas. And we venture into something that, like the image of a Tolkien forest, is likely to be dimly lit and unexplored. On many occasions in which we have worked with organizations and leaders in helping them become more innovative and spark new growth, we jokingly refer to venturing onto this creative path as "coming over to the dark side," meaning the unknown and adventuresome place of possibilities.

Organizations are all about the light and having the work they do day in and day out reflect certainty, form, and "reality." In business today, what is known is considered safe, and what is concrete is considered true. On the dark and unknown side, when our creative genius is sparked, we begin to venture into a world of abstractions, ideas, and possibilities. Venturing into the unknown may be a very exciting and scary journey, particularly as we are exposed to the glaring light of corporate judgment, which will often blur or even distort the creative sparks we are following. We may worry that when we come forth with an idea and take a risk we are putting ourselves in danger of being rejected. This is why when we have a spark moment, attach to it, and venture into it, the process of creation and manifestation makes us feel vulnerable. Not only do our own insecurities manifest themselves (Will this work? Can I really do this? I don't know what I'm doing!), but also the projections of those around us may make us feel a little sheepish. Once exposed to the light, the image you have in your mind will not necessarily look or feel the same to others in a world that values certainty, concrete ideas, precision, and explicit details. There is often very little room in the world of light for abstractions, hunches, and notions. Every characteristic and every blemish of the idea that you sparked in the security of your private world is now suddenly open to criticism and evaluation.

> *When you have come to the edge of all light that you know and are about to drop off into the darkness of the unknown, faith is knowing one of two things will happen: there will be something solid to stand on or you will be taught to fly.*
>
> —Patrick Overton, educator, poet, playwright

The challenge within organizations, and in our personal lives, is that if we desire more innovative and stimulating results we must be open and appreciate the fact that our creative genius is influenced by our willingness to explore unknown paths that lie deep within us. In the context of unleashing our creative genius, there is often a split between what our work and "enlightened" world of relationships, communities, policies, procedures, rules, and best practices provide, and what comes from the creative and unbound darkroom that is stimulated by our imagination. The tension between our desire to expose our creative genius and our desire to play it safe and stick to "reality" creates an ever-widening chasm that keeps us unsure of how to get from one side to the other without falling.

Many of the creative people we have worked with and coached have said that when they felt inspired and/or a strong desire to innovate, it was like venturing into uncharted territory. They understood that by venturing into the unknown and pursuing the path, they would assume risks, including not being able to effectively illuminate or cultivate their ideas with others.

It's a Leap of Faith

Venturing toward a path of creative expression and action, especially in the light of the workday, takes a leap of faith. Like any journey, this one has costs: we have to attach and associate ourselves with a particular idea, inspired notion, or desire. While the prize for achieving success and pursuing a creative spark may be great and holds great allure, when deciding whether or not to make the leap across the chasm between dark and light, the cost of failure is something that greatly influences our actions.

In the blockbuster movie *Indiana Jones and the Last Crusade*, the heroic character Indiana Jones is on a quest for the Holy Grail. In an effort to find a creative solution and miracle to save his dying father, he enters a dark and narrow cave. Moving farther into the cave he sees light, which leads him to a chasm. Across the deep abyss there is another cave in which a faint light glimmers. Nervous and breathing heavily, the ingenious Indiana Jones is unsure how to proceed. He hesitates and contemplates his choices for a moment, and then, in what seems like a perilous and foolhardy move, he summons his courage to step into empty air, slowly muttering to himself the words, "It's a leap of faith, a leap of faith, oh God." With one giant step, suddenly the path becomes visible and Indiana Jones is able to continue his journey.

Making a leap and venturing into unknown territory works this way. Creative genius requires bold energy and faith. Compelled by sparks of ideas and energy, we come to a point in our creative journey where it is necessary to take a leap of faith. With that, we accept that outcomes may at first be uncertain and dangerous. However, if we make the leap and relinquish our control for clarity and certainty and trust our instincts (much like our Viszla pup), we give ourselves a fighting chance to clear a path, rejoice in the experience of awakening our creative genius, and ultimately shine the light on other possibilities that will unleash it still further.

VENTURING INTO YOUR UNKNOWN

What does it mean to you to venture into the unknown?

If you knew you couldn't fail, what idea, hunch, or notion would you take into the light of the world? What is one thing that you could do right now to begin to make that a reality?

Visualize yourself having successfully achieved this. What does it feel like? What is your life like now that you've done it? What great things are happening as a result of having accomplished this?

So, what's stopping you? Start this moment to venture into your unknown and begin to illuminate your ideas!

GENIUS: To KNOW WITHOUT HAVING LEARNED; To DRAW JUST CONCLUSIONS FROM UNKNOWN PREMISES; To DISCERN THE SOUL OF THINGS.

—AMBROSE BIERCE, AMERICAN AUTHOR, WRITER, AND JOURNALIST

Getting Ready to Leap: Building Confidence and Courage

As business professionals, authors, and consultants, we work in a world in which our faith in our ideas and actions is tested time and time again. When we take a risk by suggesting a new idea and a path that we are convinced will help others grow, we know that we will be opening ourselves up to potential criticism and loss of control. After all, organizations, as we have learned, concentrate on critique and evaluation, not necessarily originality and expression. Even when innovation is considered necessary for organizational survival, private and public organizations often still value linear and well-defined actions and results above the artistic and creative expressions of their workforces. And the spotlight of creative success can be so intense that the members of the workforce don't want to deal with the attention.

Picture this: You're sitting in a meeting with your colleagues trying to brainstorm solutions to a problem. As someone gets the courage to express an idea, you hear, "That will never work," or "We've tried that before," or "No one will ever let that happen," or "We just don't do things like that here." If nothing else, these naysayers never learned the rules of brainstorming. What happened to rule number one, no judgment!?! Ignoring this rule certainly doesn't encourage more ideas to emerge from the group.

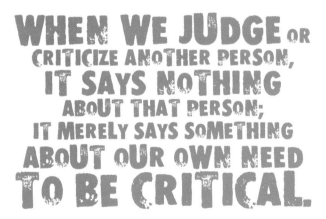

WHEN WE JUDGE or CRITICIZE ANOTHER PERSON, IT SAYS NOTHING ABOUT THAT PERSON; IT MERELY SAYS SOMETHING ABOUT OUR OWN NEED TO BE CRITICAL.

—Unknown

Venturing into an invisible creative space is a nonlinear, messy, unclear process, and it's seen by many organization leaders as an inefficient use of time that shows mixed results. Even when there is an earnest commitment

THAT WILL NEVER WORK.

WE'VE TRIED THAT BEFORE.

NO ONE WILL EVER LET THAT HAPPEN.

WE JUST DON'T DO THINGS LIKE THAT HERE.

to acquiring and generating fresh new ideas, organizations limit this approach in an effort to keep the ideation and cultivation of sparks tightly controlled. Too much ideation is seen as fluff and vaporware, not something of substance and form.

In work we nourish safe, secure, and clear actions that can be quantified, tested, and implemented. Work belongs to the realm of order and predictability, not whims, hunches, or possibilities. The many of us who experience and nurture spark moments and consciously look to exercise our creative genius often find that we have been taught to have very little faith in our ideas. And as a result, we find the habit of venturing a gamble, just as the word suggests. Very few are willing to wager their proven equity for big, new, fresh ideas.

- -

CONFIDENCE

What does confidence mean to you? What does it look like? Feel like? Sound like? Smell like? Taste like? Create a poem on confidence and incorporate your answers. Here are some examples from our workshops:

"Confidence is like a blooming flower, comes from the ground never doubting its purpose, its existence, its journey." —Marie M.

"Confidence smells like an ocean breeze—coolly, calmly, charismatically persistent." —Peter P.

"Confidence means never denying that which you know from within." —Jim H.

"Spicy to the tongue, beautiful to the eye, gentle to the touch, aromatic to the nose—confidence is." —Lori J.

- -

Oliver Wendell Holmes once said, "What lies behind us and what lies before us are tiny matters compared to what lies within us," suggesting that our real challenge lies within and is often the biggest barrier to making a leap and venturing into a more creative space. Throughout our work and life experiences we have identified several dynamics that influence whether or not we will make a leap and pursue cultivating our creative genius further.

Self-doubt

To step into the unknown requires a great deal of confidence. The opposite of confidence is self-doubt. Self-doubt is the part of creative contemplation that says, *What if people do not like what I have to suggest?* Or, *No one is likely to support my idea,* or, worse, *It's too far-fetched, so why bother even sharing it? Why should I expose myself?* Self-doubt is more concerned with impossibility and figuring out ways to defeat our inspirations than encouraging possibility and risk taking. Self-doubt feeds our fear that if we fail we will be alone and exposed and vulnerable. As we said before, organizations value and reward proven and concrete results. Therefore, feeding our creative genius and letting our imagination wander and venture is often perceived as risky.

We learn very early in life that such things as equations, theories, and ideas need proof to be accepted. Consequently, we are concerned with fitting in, staying in a space of certainty and safety rather than venturing into darker, hidden spaces of our imagination and creative passion. We are split between producing clear, tangible, concrete results and pursuing, cultivating, and experimenting with the faint renderings that have been playing out in our minds. The state of our creative genius and whether we break out and venture into unknown territory depends on our willingness to take risks and accept failure as one of the possibilities.

YOUR CURRENT SAFE BOUNDARIES WERE ONCE UNKNOWN FRONTIERS.

—UNKNOWN

When we asked Rick Dzavik, the former European innovation leader for a large consumer health-care company, if he ever had any doubts about his success and ability to obtain support for his innovation agenda, he smiled and said, "Every day. From the moment we began to conceive and shape a program for building a more innovative culture to actually implementing one, my team and I would frequently question our own actions and even went as far as not trusting our intuition on things because of past experiences. It took a long time to hit our stride, but eventually, as we gained traction, we improved our level of confidence." Of course, Dzavik and his team were hugely successful, even though they still had some doubts along the way. So keep in mind that when you're contemplating whether or not to venture into unknown places, things may feel beyond your reach, similar to Indiana Jones looking across the chasm. It may at first be daunting, but you won't know until you ultimately make the leap.

Growth means change and change involves risk, stepping from the known to the unknown.
—UNKNOWN

In work today the stakes are increasingly high. Because of increased competition, high-performance targets, and the vicissitude associated with corporate takeovers and layoffs, our desire and willingness to venture out is shaky at best. And in general, as John Lennon sang so eloquently, "Life is what happens to you while you're busy making other plans," causing you to react and shift your priorities. Without notice, your husband one day declares to you that he hates his job and quits, or your boss informs you that your services are no longer needed and you are out of a job. The emphasis on the bottom line and constant pressure to produce in most modern jobs often make the human psyche the ball in a ping-pong match between our desire to operate in artistic, self-expressive ways and our need to conform to the realities of the corporate stage and associated spotlights of tried-and-true behaviors. We want to express ourselves and unleash our creative flow, but we easily give in to self-doubt and retreat into safe behaviors when we need to make a decision or commit to a course of action.

Have you ever had a spark of an idea but suppressed it as quickly as it came to you because of your lack of confidence? Our creative streams are often dammed by a combination of self-doubt and the unconscious, bland expectations of other people and our organizations. Work is perceived as a place of sweat and toil where little or no time is devoted to attracting or advancing energy to creative thought. As a result, we avoid taking the step to release that vital creative spirit we are born with, opting instead to keep it safe and hidden in the dark recesses of our minds.

CREATIVE GENIUS CHALLENGE

The next time you have a spark and hesitate to share it with someone else, either at work or at home, imagine that they will not only not judge or criticize it, but instead fully embrace it and help you to realize the spark's full potential! Then go ahead and share it!

THERE IS NOTHING MORE DREADFUL THAN THE HABIT OF DOUBT. DOUBT SEPARATES PEOPLE. IT IS A POISON THAT DISINTEGRATES FRIENDSHIPS AND BREAKS UP PLEASANT RELATIONS. IT IS A THORN THAT IRRITATES AND HURTS; IT IS A SWORD THAT KILLS.

—SIDDHARTHA GAUTAMA, FOUNDER OF BUDDHISM

"It takes too much time and effort to think out of the box," a medical researcher once said to us, "because of the constant pressure to make money and deliver results." Maybe you can relate to this. We know what you're up against. We know it's not easy. We also know that in order to access your creative genius, you must no longer let that hold you back. To express yourself creatively means to make yourself vulnerable to accepting that naked and sometimes lonely feeling associated with bringing forth an idea into the light where everyone can see it, prod it, and poke holes in it. Judgment is one of the many spotlights we may endure when we call forth a creative spark from our darkroom. If we are not ready or don't have the courage to receive the potential scrutiny, then we are doomed to feeling overexposed and vulnerable. To venture forth and make a leap into the unknown requires a great deal of faith and trust in the journey.

Checking Your Creative Genius at the Door

Has your mind ever wandered during your morning commute to the office and you've found yourself suddenly thinking of new possibilities, opportunities, and ideas that could result in more success for your organization or lead to greater fulfillment in your life? The dream is sometimes so clear and so wonderful that you feel invincible and convinced that you may be on to something very special. And then, just as you're walking into the building where you work, your spirit weakens and the spark flickers and then fades out entirely. Without a second thought, you checked your creative muses at the door, suspending your dreamlike state in favor of reality, certainty, predictability, and routine. From the moment you got situated in your workspace, you immediately found yourself barraged by e-mails, meetings, to-do lists, reports, and presentations. What happened to all that creative energy you had moments ago? It quickly dissipated into tiny particles that got sucked up into the dry and stale environment of your office.

Life happens, schedules take over, and you find yourself enslaved by the comfort and shelter of your office, which, if it is like most offices, is probably an almost antiseptic environment devoid of much artistic and creative venturing. As your day begins, it seems that as soon as you complete one task you are on to another, with no time for your mind to wander or advance the ideas and creative energy that were emerging earlier in your day. You're not necessarily looking for possibility, you're just hoping to slog through the day, get through what you need to get through in order to simply survive. Surviving is okay, but what about thriving?

IT TAKES **BUT ONE POSITIVE THOUGHT... GIVEN A CHANCE TO SURVIVE AND THRIVE TO OVERPOWER AN ENTIRE ARMY OF NEGATIVE THOUGHTS.**

—ROBERT SCHULLER,
MINISTER, ENTREPRENEUR, AUTHOR

In *The Heart Aroused: Poetry and the Preservation of Soul in Corporate America*, David Whyte discusses the struggle workers have in adapting their creative spirits to their work. Throughout his provocative and compelling book, Whyte suggests that we must embrace our careers with both heart and mind. If the time is right for employing our creative spirits in order to grow personally and innovate organizationally, then we must open up to what Whyte calls "a mature appreciation of the hidden and often dangerous inner seas where our passions and our creativity lie waiting." Much of our time spent in work pulls us away from our creative genius, confining our attention to matters more mundane and leaving us empty in environments that are, in Whyte's words, "dehydrated."

The secret to unlocking your creative genius and permitting yourself to venture off and run with a creative impulse is akin to what we infer from Dante's *The Divine Comedy*: awaken your soul to act. *The Divine Comedy* is based on Dante's own experiences as a political exile for two years from his home in Florence. He describes his exile as a form of hell—an inferno of death stripping him of all that he treasured and valued most, his soul and his creative expression: "You shall leave everything you love most dearly: this is the arrow that the bow of exile shoots first. You are to know the bitter taste of others' bread, how salty it is, and know how hard a path it is for one who goes ascending and descending others' stairs."

Your spirits and creative expression may remain dark and live in exile in your linear world of work unless you consciously seek to awaken that part of who you are. But it's not easy to venture into a creative state of mind, especially since the world values and rewards the opposite. Rather than live in exile, take your creative genius with you wherever you go and feel confident in your ideas and abilities. Consciously bringing your creative muses with you wherever you go will do more than just get you through the day—it will keep you thriving.

> *You have to leave the city of your comfort and go into the wilderness of your intuition. What you'll discover will be wonderful. What you'll discover is yourself.*
>
> —ALAN ALDA, AMERICAN ACTOR

CREATIVE GENIUS CHALLENGE

Look through your closet and drawers and try to find an article of clothing or an accessory that will add a little spark to your day, keep you stimulated, and remind you to keep your creative energy flowing all day, every day. You can find something of interest hiding like a buried treasure deep in your closets or other places, waiting to be rediscovered and used. If you can't find anything you think will stimulate you, buy something new and wear it tomorrow!

Succumbing to Appearances

Awakening and bringing our venturing spirit into our work and our daily lives comes at a price. We must be willing to shed our professional attire, often figuratively and sometimes literally, and don the wardrobe of more creative work that often is messy and inexact. However, as we've said, everything about organizations is about precision, uniformity, and conformity. The reason we are often afraid to venture down the unknown paths of creativity is that we succumb to concern over appearances.

In our work, we playfully talk about clothing and the importance of being in a relaxed state in order to be more creative. We poke some fun at the tradition of wearing neckties and suggest that they restrict the blood flow to our heads, which in turn leads to low levels of creative thinking. There is still a widely held belief among organizations today that wearing a suit makes you more credible and more productive. Adhering to such beliefs, we believe, especially in the sweltering days of summer, seems a little over the top. We are happy to see that organizations are beginning to relax such conformity in favor of more casual attire. But the big question is, is the result more creativity?

While we are using clothing to illustrate a point, the threat to creativity from appearance is not limited to what we wear. It's more than that. Trapped beneath dress codes, policies, reviews, and performance evaluations, individual expressions are just not welcome in some organizations. We once worked with the head of global innovation for a large retailer who was specifically charged with bringing in a more innovative work ethic and spurring product- and service-related innovations. Despite his previous successes and world-renowned reputation for innovation, within months of his arrival he was "coached" about his appearance because he wore black jeans on a consistent basis. Just between us, you could barely tell that they were jeans in the first place! Casual, maybe, but he was hardly unkempt. We believe the jeans were his subtle way of not conforming, of choosing to be more comfortable, especially since his role was to encourage others to cultivate their creative side. The

CAN YOU THINK MORE CREATIVELY IN SNEAKERS?

jeans were a nonverbal cue that things were going to be done differently, and doing things differently was what he was hired to do. However, because he wore jeans he was politely chastised and told not to be so casual. "Not cool," he was told. All in the name of conformity—heaven forbid that some deviate from the norm.

Standing at the edge of uncharted territory, you really only have two choices, to pass on the hunch or idea and retreat back to safe land or lunge forward to the side of possibility full force and with gusto.

—IAN CAMPBELL, PROJECT MANAGER,
A LEADING NATIONAL GENERAL
CONTRACTING COMPANY

Organizations are living, evolving entities, and yet the ways we attempt to organize and manage them would seem to suggest they are stiff and static bodies in which everyone must perform in a strict and robotic fashion, devoid of individual expression. If we are to encourage our creative genius and allow people to venture into creative possibilities, then we must embrace more fluid, playful conditions—even those that break from the norm—in order to spark new possibilities. Rather than seeing an organization as a house of conformity where consistency and sameness rule the day, the appearance of creativity should be suggested in the passion, spontaneity, and individual expression that are accepted and nurtured throughout the company. The context in which we expect people to bring their creative energies into the workplace must be absolutely considered. We've already explored the importance of conditions and environment in chapter 4, but to reiterate a key point, fidelity to rules, especially those that stifle individual expression, will not guarantee a productive and creative organization.

WHAT'S GETTING IN THE WAY OF YOUR CREATIVE GENIUS?

According to Jim Rohn, motivational speaker, philosopher, and entrepreneur, there are five fears that get in the way of our success. What's interesting about all of these fears is that they come from within. That is, we create these fears in our mind, but our mind can also be used as a powerful tool to change them. Which fears do you relate to?

- **Indifference**: apathy, lack of motivation or enthusiasm
- **Indecision**: unsureness, wavering, irresolution
- **Doubt**: hesitation, uncertainty
- **Worry**: anxiousness, fretting, concern
- **Overcaution**: timidity, overguardedness, tentativeness

The following exercise may help you use the power of your mind to overcome these self-imposed fears. Fold a piece of paper in half. On one side, draw a picture of yourself with the fear or fears from the list above that you relate to. Next, on the other side of the paper, draw yourself without this fear (or fears). What's different? How does the side without the fears feel? What steps could you take to become more like the person depicted in the image?

On the Edge of a Leap

Before making a leap you may be overcome by anxiety and fear. Realize that the anticipation of a leap is sometimes more challenging than finally committing to one course of action or another. If you decide to venture into the unknown by bringing things to light, it can be one of the most exciting moments you ever experience. "Standing at the edge

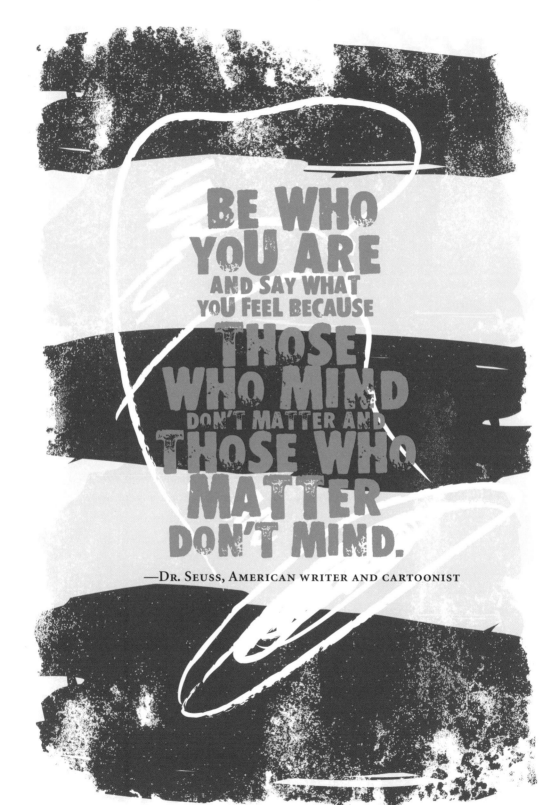

BE WHO
YOU ARE
AND SAY WHAT
YOU FEEL BECAUSE
THOSE
WHO MIND
DON'T MATTER AND
THOSE WHO
MATTER
DON'T MIND.

—Dr. Seuss, American writer and cartoonist

of uncharted territory," says Ian Campbell, product manager for a large construction company, "is both scary and exhilarating at the same time." Fond of exploring new ground, Campbell feels that when you have a spark you really only have two choices: "pass on the hunch or idea and retreat back to safe land or lunge forward to the side of possibility full force and with gusto."

To bring your creative expression out from under the covers of darkness you must trust your instincts. It's that simple. Developing the courage and support network to do so is another matter. Reaching the other side of the chasm requires not only belief in yourself but skill as well. Christopher Columbus, the extraordinary explorer and sailor, was both a visionary and an individual skilled in human dynamics. For a long time he contemplated and conducted research, including studying the travels of Marco Polo and examining the maps of Egyptian astronomers such as Ptolemy. He was also astute in the subtleties of communication. He knew that in order to advance his vision he would need the sponsorship of the leaders of Spain. Through his ability to mimic the aristocratic dialect, he was able to engender trust and confidence in the nobles he approached. With an "anything is possible" attitude and the skills to make it happen, Columbus made a leap into an unknown adventure that now is part of history. Do you think Columbus had any fears or doubts? Especially when the predominant belief at the time was that the world was flat and once you hit the edge, you'd fall off? No doubt he had his fears, but he did it anyway. Columbus had a vision *and* he had the ability and courage to make the leap.

So, how might we be Columbus-like and overcome our fears? We must be stimulated by the vision we want and move forward with the confidence that we will transcend the gaps and crevices that will undoubtedly be a part of the journey—we must align our heads and our hearts and drive forward with perseverance and confidence. And, of course, we must discover what skills we need, and acquire them.

Passion and Practicality

We recently went to a musical festival where many different exhibitors were selling materials or displaying their crafts while musicians performed onstage. One booth focused on Tai Chi, the ancient martial art aimed at promoting lifelong health. On display was an object (presumably filled with herbs) intended to be placed on a person's head to either remove a headache or prevent a headache from developing. The young woman who demonstrated how the object is used talked generally about the practice of Tai Chi, and discussed the importance of maintaining a cool head and keeping the fire in the belly. "If you have a headache, you likely have too much heat percolating up into your brain, and you need to move the excess heat, which you feel in the form of tension, back toward your abdomen."

What she said made complete sense. To us the significance was less in terms of the expression "fire in the belly" and more to do with what Kouzes and Posner, experts on the topic of leadership, wrote about twenty years ago: the importance of encouraging the heart. The key to producing fiery results comes from the exchange between our hearts and our minds, that which we are passionate about and that which is practical. How well we stoke the chambers of passion in the heart while keeping the mind cool determines not only the success of our ideas but our courage to act upon them. "From a little spark may burst a flame," wrote Dante, suggesting that all we need is one spark to stimulate our creative passion and encourage us to pursue things that we value and want to create.

A spark of heat plays a dual relationship. On the one hand, heat provides us with warmth and energy; on the other hand, if we get too close to a heat source we may get burned: we get so wrapped up in our passion that we fail to see the practical side of things. So as we contemplate pursuing our creative impulses and venture into the unknown with passion and practicality, we must do as Columbus did, go forth with an awareness of vision but also understanding the importance of gathering resources in order to be successful. He had to influence the aristocracy of Spain before he could venture out into the open sea. Engendering the support of the leaders is a perfect illustration of the balance between our head and our hearts. He had a fire in his belly, but he used his head to help realize his vision. We need both our heart and our mind to work harmoniously together to make the leap.

YOUR VISION WILL BECOME CLEAR ONLY WHEN YOU LOOK INTO YOUR HEART . . . WHO LOOKS OUTSIDE DREAMS, WHO LOOKS INSIDE AWAKENS.

—CARL JUNG, SWISS PSYCHIATRIST

Being in touch with the dynamic nature of our creative fires helps us to successfully manage our passions while practically pursuing a path that will help us navigate uncharted waters.

Most of us have a tendency to keep our creative thoughts and spirits hidden safely within our minds, on the "dark side." But as we said earlier, creative venturing involves attaching to sparks that become a source of creative heat, which in turn helps to ignite our passion and illuminate our genius, bringing it into full view. So the habit of venturing and making the leap is really an outward expression of the energy that at first may be stimulated inwardly through our scouting, cultivating, and playing habits. As the resolution of your ideas becomes clear in your mind, the time for exposing them should follow naturally. The habit of venturing is a process of "creating out," like speaking out, making known what it is you envision, seek, are all charged up about, and want to make a reality.

While your own fiery passions for creative expression may lie within and the fear of being burnt by the intense rays of reality may inhibit you from making the leap, any time you take steps toward venturing into new, fresh paths rich with possibilities, the universe will seem to rearrange itself to support your journey.

—WILLIAM JAMES,
AMERICAN PSYCHOLOGIST
AND PHILOSOPHER

Profiles in Venturing

We'd like to share a few stories of some people we have either heard from or heard about who ventured into the unknown and took a leap that positively affected their lives. What's neat about these stories is that they show that sometimes by design, sometimes by default, life takes us in certain directions that we may not expect. When opportunities present themselves for us to make the leap, we need to choose: will we leap or will we lie?

"I wasn't sure how I was going to do it, but knew for my own [sanity] and the sanity of my family, I had no choice. I had a secure job as an administrative assistant and while I loved what I did, it just didn't allow me to be fully me. I began a business that allows me to be at home with my children after school yet gives me the creative outlet to be engaged in the work I am passionate about and live for."

—ARLENE T.,
married, mother of three

"I was let go from
my corporate job just as I was
initiating other serious life changes.
I was unhappy in my job, and it must
have shown. Just when I thought I needed
the security of this corporate job, especially
as I was going about rearranging my personal
world, I was dumbfounded when my boss called
me into his office that morning. In retrospect, it
was the best thing that could have ever happened
to me. Now not only am I pursuing my passion, but I'm actually getting paid for it! It's
wild. Never would I have thought that I
would be doing what I love to do. I had to
make the leap, accepting that
it was okay to do some-
thing other than what
I had always done. It
was not only okay—it
was a necessity."

—JOHN P., happily exiled corporate executive

Victoria Knight-McDowell, through her actions, embodies the venturing spirit. The teacher who was "sick of getting sick" in her California classroom founded the best-selling herbal suite of products called Airborne. Chances are, you've seen her product in supermarkets and drugstores and perhaps even tested it out. As reported in O, The Oprah Magazine, in September 2005, she says that over a conversation at dinner one night with her husband, "it just sort of flowed until we said, 'let's put it on the market and see what happens.'" After depleting their retirement and savings funds to "make the leap," they hand-labeled 12,000 bottles and made sales calls after school. Probably what we love most about her story is how she dealt with the all-too-familiar naysayers that we spoke of earlier. Says Knight-McDowell, "When we were starting out, our friends and family thought we should invest in a house instead of Airborne." She advises others on what to do if you encounter people who don't support your dream or idea. She says, "People will say, 'Oh, what a crazy idea!' or 'You can't do that.' You have to ignore them." Cheers to that!

—**VICTORIA KNIGHT-MCDOWELL,**
wife, mother, and owner of Airborne Products

PEOPLE WHO SAY
IT CANNOT BE DONE
SHOULD NOT
INTERRUPT
THOSE WHO ARE DOING IT.
—Unknown

Venturing: The Oxygen for Your Ideas

If you are serious about making the leap, then you must make venturing into the unknown a habit. The irony is that while your creative embers will spark in your dark chambers, in order for you to realize the full potential of your creative self, you must create out, bring forth, and make known your ideas to others. Instead of keeping them in the dark, you must bring them to light. Plato once said that "you can easily forgive a child who is afraid of the dark but not an adult who is afraid of the light." When we decide to venture and attach to a spark and fan it further so that it may catch fire, then we accept that what creative expression needs most is the validation of light and energy from others. Just as oxygen keeps a fire alive, the input, reactions, and expression of others can and should positively impact the expression of the ideas that you have sparking within. If you keep your ideas and sparks to yourself and never take a risk, their flame will eventually burn out, and if left uncultivated, all sparks of creative expression will ultimately become extinguished—certainly not the goal of a path toward creative genius. When we feel that burning desire to express our creative genius, we each must confront one essential question: Do I keep it silent and dim where no one can see it or do I let it come bursting out in hopes that it may catch fire and blaze a new path of adventure and possibility? If the answer to that question is yes, you will keep sparking and bringing ideas to the light.

DID YOU KNOW

Did you know that women start 424 new enterprises every day?
Did you know that 600,000 new businesses are started each year? That's lots of people making a leap!

Life is either a daring adventure or nothing.

—HELEN KELLER, AMERICAN AUTHOR,
ACTIVIST, AND LECTURER

TIPS FOR VENTURING

- Be confident and courageous.
- Change the way you think about what others might think.
- Visualize success with whatever your spark is; feel how it will feel when you are successful!
- Do something about that spark you have right now! Do something that propels you into action, conduct research, call a friend, sketch out a plan. Just one baby step is all it takes!
- Don't worry about the opinions of others—trust your intuition.
- Ditch doubt—along with ties and sensible shoes!
- Eliminate fear for good; it doesn't serve you.
- Work with the law of attraction: think about what you want, ask for it to be, and expect that it will come. Know that anything is possible.
- Become an advocate for others' ideas. Be supportive!
- Trust your instincts.
- Take your creative energy everywhere you go!
- Keep your head cool and the fire in your belly.

Chapter 7

Real Results:
Harvesting Creative Action

Okay, we admit it, we're addicted to HGTV, Home and Garden Television. Each year we are convinced that we are going to be one of the lucky winners among millions who participate in the network's Dream Home Contest. One year the prize was a house in North Carolina. We were absolutely certain that we were going to win the big prize right up to the moment the awards were announced. Unfortunately we never got the call. Nonetheless, the clever programming and interactive nature of the contest really got us hooked. We became fast fans, and we suspect our behavior was not so unique—likely one of the many reasons why HGTV is such a huge success. HGTV, which is run by Scripps Networks, is one of the fastest-growing and most successful brands for television and the Internet. Thanks to Scripps Networks and a plethora of creative pioneers, the new "synchronous programming" model is really hot in TV and related media industries. It has transformed an industry that was exclusively about pushing information to the audience into one that is more engaging and interactive with the audience.

Among the many bright and talented innovators who are responsible for producing original TV at Scripps Networks, Channing Dawson,

DEDICATED
PERSISTENT
STEADFAST

PURPOSEFUL
TRUE

HARMONIOUS
PRODUCTIVE

WHOLEHEARTED
VIABLE
GENERATIVE

#5
*HARVESTING

senior vice president of New Ventures, was recruited to harvest new programming like HGTV and leverage content. Dawson is always thinking, musing, and conjuring up some exciting and stimulating ideas. In short, he's not your typical buttoned-down business executive who will bore you with business plans and financial details. Rather, he will keep you spellbound with grand visions of 3D technology and how it can both entertain you and provide you with useful information. While occasionally glancing out at his Knoxville office as if he were searching for the next big idea, Dawson, a self-proclaimed scout, also possesses a keen ability to cultivate, play with, and venture forth with new ideas to harvest real results.

WHAT WE PLANT IN THE SOIL OF CONTEMPLATION, WE SHALL REAP IN THE HARVEST OF ACTION.

—MEISTER ECKHART, GERMAN WRITER AND THEOLOGIAN

In our parlance, we define "harvesting" as the consequence of all our creative activities (scouting, cultivating, playing, and venturing) that advances spark moments into real results. The "harvest" is the sum total or yield of all of our efforts, and the celebration of those results. It is transforming your sparks into ideas that not only become real and tangible, but also stimulate more sparks and ideas. Many people have great spark moments, but seldom do they act upon them and set aside the time to grow them into real creative results. After scouting, cultivating, and playing in order to attract sparks and venturing to commit to a spark and make the leap, you put yourself in a position of harvesting and yielding many wonderful and inspired results both personally and professionally. The more frequently you complete this cycle, the more confident you are in your creative genius and the more ready you are to sow and transform other sparks into productive and creative results. The key is to take the sparks that you attracted and committed to and develop them into tangible and inspiring ideas that lead to creative, successful results. This can be accomplished through passion, creative harmony, and celebration.

THE **ONLY WAY** YOU CAN BRING IN **THE HARVEST IN THE FALL** IS TO **PLANT IN THE SPRING** AND TO **WATER AND WEED AND** FERTILIZE IN THE **SUMMER.**

—UNKNOWN

Harvesting Spark Moments to Yield Stimulating Outcomes

Creative harvesting is not only making real the sparks and ideas you have come up with as a result of your creative journey, but also stimulating other possibilities. In other words, harvesting means bringing into concrete existence sparks and ideas and in doing so opening your creative genius to encourage more sparks. Ideas are like crops that represent the total yield of all of our creative energies and habits. Once a fertile and creative foundation is put in place through the habits of scouting, cultivating, playing, and venturing, we are ready to begin harvesting our ideas into real results that more often than not will spark other new possibilities. So, for example, if someone has an idea for a new product that emerged through one of the other creative habits. such as playing, the development of the product and advancement of the product into reality is the act of harvesting. The more ideas we harvest, the bigger our bounty for stimulating outcomes will be. The process of harvesting completes the cycle of sparking your creative genius.

Don't judge each day by the harvest you reap
but by the seeds that you plant.

—ROBERT LOUIS STEVENSON, SCOTTISH ESSAYIST AND POET

At the onset of sparking our creative genius—the moment we feel stimulated—our hearts and minds erupt with renewed life and anticipation just as the earth reawakens in the spring from its long winter slumber. Our first attempt at producing creative results, however, may still be fragile from the freshness of our spark. As soon as we feel the heat of our passion rising, our spark moments begin to take root in the form of distinct ideas. All of a sudden one idea after another begins sprouting up, curling its way up from deep inside the dark ground, slowly responding and tipping toward the direction of our energy, motivation, and passion. The spark has piqued our interest and we are engaged and hungry for more. The time to give our sparks attention and light is now. Sparks take on heliotropic qualities, meaning they seek energy similar to how plants seek sun for their growth. The more energy we give to sparks, the more likely that the "stem tip" of our ideas will have a chance to grow into something of substance. Harvesting your sparks and ideas means you are leaving your mark and producing stimulating, real outcomes.

You must give to get, you must sow the seed
before you can reap the harvest.

—UNKNOWN

NURTURE CREATE THE OPPORTUNITY FOR
YOUR CREATIVE SPIRIT GROWTH
GERMINATION IS THE FIRST STAGE OF
GROWTH CREATIVITY
REQUIRES THE RIGHT CONDITIONS
YOU MUST BREAK THROUGH THE STAGE OF SEEDLINGS WILL ONLY GROW WHEN
DORMANCY IT'S TIME
WITHIN EACH SEED, WITHIN EACH OF US, IS A HIDDEN ABUNDANCE OF
STORED ENERGY

CREATIVE GENIUS CHALLENGE

What sprout of an idea is ready for you to harvest? What's one thing you can do today to reap the benefits of this idea?

Harvesting stimulating outcomes represents a cycle of activity that continuously puts us in the frame of mind to advance ideas, seek abundance, and keep working until we create something of value or something concrete.

The results you achieve will be in direct proportion to the effort you apply.
  —DENIS WAITLEY, MOTIVATIONAL SPEAKER

HGTV: Harvesters Hard at Work

The seeds of creativity at the amazing Scripps Networks were first germinated by the vision and passion of Ken Lowe, CEO. Lowe grew up in rural North Carolina and was enthralled by radio at an early age. By the time he reached his teens he had built a small radio station with broadcasting power that could only reach a few miles and an audience that he humorously recalls as being a "few chickens, cows, and supportive neighbors." Passionate about radio and creating pictures with words, Lowe joined Scripps in 1980 as a general manager, quickly rising to become chairman and CEO. At Scripps he pulled together a formidable team of TV, media, and journalism professionals to produce various cable network–driven TV. He is also responsible for "synchronous programming," real-time programming in which a viewer, while watching a show, is given information (or the viewer can click on the television to obtain additional information) about featured products. In addition to the widely successful HGTV, Lowe and his team of innovators also created DIY and Shop at Home networks.

Reflecting on the success of HGTV, Channing Dawson recalls that they did a lot of "bootstrapping of the basics" just to get the concept off the ground. Launched in late 1994, HGTV was not expected to be successful because it was an independent production/media company that had no experience in the cable networking business. Scripps is comprised mainly of journalists and programming professionals steeped in the experiences and best practices of entertainment, reporting information, stories, and content. Facing a very competitive landscape and not knowing much about the cable business, Scripps decided, under the able leadership from Dawson and the compelling vision from Lowe, to fund the first investment. "We didn't have a marketing department when we first launched the programming so my team and I believed it was important to plant our creative energies into the programming, which was our strength," said Dawson. So, unlike other television networks that licensed content from producers, Scripps decided to own the content. "The genesis of Ken [Lowe]'s idea was to have me incubate the supporting ideas that would make HGTV into an evergreen enterprise with the capability of continuously repurposing content while improving upon our programming strength."

QUALITY QUESTIONS CREATE A QUALITY LIFE. SUCCESSFUL PEOPLE ASK BETTER QUESTIONS AND AS A RESULT GET BETTER ANSWERS.

—ANTHONY ROBBINS,
MOTIVATIONAL SPEAKER, ENTREPRENEUR

Dawson and his colleagues at Scripps raised some big questions first before investing in strategies that he described as "proselytizing" their product. During their first foray into the cable network business, Scripps's objective was to portray to the viewer the experience of the character on the program and his or her actions featured during the episode. For example, the actual remodeling a couple did on their home was emphasized, not the products they used to help them remodel the home. However, as they began to informally produce various programming, Dawson and others began to question how they could provide information about products without necessarily compromising the essence of their business. Based on the early exploration efforts that highlighted a trend toward more interactive TV, Dawson further investigated how they might own database television. Having come out of the magazine world, Dawson was accustomed to leveraging the relationship with subscribers and converting them into long-term buyers. However, unlike periodicals, TV did not have a database to leverage—that was something owned by the cable networks, such as Comcast and Time Warner.

Relentless in his pursuit of what we refer to as "making it real," Dawson began to figure out ways to get their programming audience to call or contact the network. He elaborates, "The genesis of the idea was if we could get our audience to get in touch with us then we would have some way of databasing their information. And if we could database their information then we could repurpose the data in many stimulating and profitable ways." This effort led to the idea of setting up a call center viewers could contact for information on products used during programming. It was the first of its kind among the TV channels and producers who were competing with HGTV.

"When we decided to do the call center and got that up and running," said Dawson, "one innovation led to another and it was clear that the best thing about it was that we were actually talking to our users, and we could pick their brain." Dawson knew very quickly after some informal testing and validating that they were on to a new creative habit in their industry. They heard things from their viewers like "I am addicted to your network because you provide me with some content and other valuable resources to help me remodel my home."

"As we began to interact with our audience," said Dawson, "we were able to reap big results based on the efforts and the zeitgeist of our industry." The bounty Scripps Networks produced resulted in higher ratings and audience responses and fundamentally transformed how television was being viewed. Up until that point television had been seen as a media tool, not an interactive, communicative experience. The bias in the television industry, according to Dawson, "has always been about programmers pushing their ideas down to the audience and seeing if the audience likes it. We marked the beginning of this new season of synchronous programming as soon as we began to introduce this approach. Coupled with advancements in the web, we were able to produce whole new ways of recasting our data."

I SEE POSSIBILITIES
AND I SHOW UP;
I HAVE FUN AND I AM ENGAGED;
I QUESTION AND
I OPEN THE SPACE
FOR LEARNING; I MULTI-SENSE
AND I REMEMBER;
I DO AND I UNDERSTAND;
I REFLECT AND INTEGRATE AND
I CAN SHARE WITH OTHERS;
I APPLY TO REAL LIFE AND
I GET RESULTS.

—Joyce Wyckoff, cofounder,
Innovation Network

The idea was brilliant. Without compromising their programming ethic of not advertising products disruptively, they were able to provide product information through the call center and thus increase ratings. "The call center did several things," Dawson said. "One, it sparked our producers to change their production guidelines to include more information in the shoot." For example, when filming a kitchen they would include detailed information about a specific set of featured appliances. "Secondly, it enabled us to put the data about products or architects into a database to equip our customer service representatives to be ready and able to respond to audience questions. This outcome then stimulated other outcomes that produced other possibilities. We put in a 1-800 number and within the first month of our launch we were inundated with calls inquiring about the products we would use in our programming."

All the flowers of tomorrow are in the seeds of today.
—Unknown

By continuously harvesting sparks and ideas, Dawson and his Scripps cohorts developed a habit of producing many different innovations that changed the landscape of TV broadcasting by shifting the medium from programming to synchronous engagement.

Creativity is the power to connect the seemingly unconnected.
—William Plomer, South African author

Once we decide to venture into possibilities and advance our sparks, like Lowe, Dawson, and others at Scripps Networks committed to producing changes in the TV and entertainment industry, then we give ourselves the chance to leave our mark. As soon as Dawson and others saw one seed of an idea that had potential for growth sprout, they mobilized others and rallied around different concepts and ideas until they produced a vast array of possibilities that ultimately helped the network become a leader in its industry.

Passion

Logan Pearsall Smith, the son of the prominent Quaker Robert Pearsall Smith, said, "There are two things to aim at in life: the first, to get what you want; and after that, to enjoy it." Harvesting stimulating outcomes should be an enjoyable process and represent the outward manifestation of our creative spirit. As we've discussed earlier, when we are passionate about what we want and we enjoy the result of our efforts we are going to be more motivated to harvest stimulating results. This does not mean the pursuit will be easy, nor does it mean we will always have fun. But generally speaking, pursuing your creative sparks and ideas with passion is an essential characteristic of producing stimulating outcomes. Passion has the mark of our creative genius all over it—in the pleasure afforded to the creator and the output of the expression. If we are inspired to create, we are likely to feel stimulated and also stimulate our relationships, efforts, and products.

Back in the early '90s, Andrew had the privilege of sitting down with Ron Trzcinski, the president of the Original Mattress Factory in Cleveland, Ohio. Andrew spent time talking to Trzcinski about how he created and inspired his organization to grow at record rates in an industry that is generally not considered especially passionate or creative. After all, what is so different about one mattress company from another? According to Trzcinski, the differences are many.

In 1990, Trzcinski and his partners started the Original Mattress Factory in order to manufacture high-quality mattresses and box springs, to provide a product of value and excellence. He started the company approximately six months after he left the Ohio Mattress Company (now known as Sealy, Inc.), which was acquired in a leveraged buyout. Trzcinski declined offers from the new owners of Ohio Mattress, because he did not

PASSION = STIMULATING RESULTS

want to be a part of their "cash is king" philosophy. "The new company's attitudes and business philosophies had no appeal to me whatsoever," recalls Trzcinski. "I did not want to work for an organization that was only concerned about making money. I am not saying money is evil; however, my passion extends well beyond money—I love to create ways to meet and exceed my customers' expectations, and I am passionate about having all of my colleagues find meaning and value in what they do."

After the leveraged buyout and some serious soul searching, Trzcinski decided to form his own mattress company. He sought to create an organization that reflected his passion for customers by removing the middleman to reduce costs and ensuring the highest-quality mattress could be produced and delivered. "I sought to sell directly to customers and create a fulfilling workplace for my colleagues as well," said Trzcinski. Within a short period of time, the Original Mattress Company expanded to include eleven factories and more than eighty factory stores. According to Trzcinski, "Sports and business are a lot alike: profit is a report card. However, I don't sit in my factory and say, 'How can we make a profit?' I ask, 'How can we do a better job of serving our customers, helping them see value and make a better bed?'" This passionate sentiment is reflected in the company principles that Trzcinski and his partners created more than twenty years ago. It still serves as the foundation for stimulating results in an industry that is often asleep and lifeless in terms of quality and customer service.

We strive for excellence in all we do. In everything we do, we should try to do the best possible job for our customers and the company. Whatever the job, there is always room for improvement, whether it be working faster, friendlier, smarter, or more economically.

We will not compromise our integrity for any reason. Nothing will come before integrity. We will always do what we say and say only what is true.

We are built on value. Think of yourself as a customer. You buy from companies that sell products that you perceive to be a good value, that treat you with respect and courtesy, that tell you the truth, and that handle any problem fairly. You judge the company by its people. If you get a rude, nasty clerk at a store, you don't want to go back to that store, even though they may spend huge amounts of time, money, and energy on every other phase of their business. Our customers are like you. No matter how much time, money, and energy we spend, if they are not treated right by us, they won't remain our customers. Without customers, none of us have a job.

We create a win-win situation in everything we do. This has to do with our dealings with customers, fellow workers, suppliers, or anyone else. It requires courage and consideration, courage to pursue a win for you, and consideration toward the other party so they can also win.

—Original Mattress Factory

I ONCE HEARD PROFIT IS THE APPLAUSE YOU GET FOR TAKING CARE OF CUSTOMERS AND YOUR PEOPLE.

—Ken Blanchard, author, speaker

Years ago we had the opportunity to do some work for an organization in Germany. Our client had arranged for a car service to pick us up once we had landed. Travel-weary after the long flight across the Atlantic, we grabbed our bags and headed out to find our driver. We spotted Heiko almost immediately, and he helped us with our luggage and escorted us to his car. The trip to the castle where we would be living and working for the next week and a half was about an hour's drive, and that was with Heiko driving as fast as he dared. Since we had the following day off, we asked Heiko for recommendations for things to do in the area. He told us he'd be happy to come back and take us to his hometown and show us around.

And so he did. The next morning Heiko drove us to a small village with picturesque buildings, charming streets, and a river winding through it. It was beautiful, and Heiko was a great tour guide. We got to know him and discovered that he wanted to help others any way he could. In fact, his motto was "I want your problems." When he dropped us off at the castle that evening, he told us to call him if we needed anything.

The next day, as we got ready for our event, we realized that the materials we had shipped before we left had not arrived. We desperately needed PowerPoint slides printed in color and bound in a workbook for over fifty participants, and we needed it done quickly! We were in a remote, very small town with few businesses of any kind, much less a Kinko's on the corner. We had no transportation and wouldn't have known where to go even if we had. As we were trying to figure out what to do, of course we thought of Heiko. Didn't he say he wanted our problems? Well, this was certainly a problem!

Within minutes Heiko had found a woman who ran a business from her home and had all the necessary materials and technical expertise to pull off what we needed in the short time frame we had. We were relieved to then be able to focus our energy and attention on getting ready for our workshop.

Heiko demonstrated real passion for his mission to help others with their problems. As the week progressed, he went on to help us find toys for a subsequent session and a pizza place to eat at one night when we were exhausted from work and unable to eat one more rich, delicious, gourmet dinner at the castle. When we and the team we were working with got wise to the castle chef repeatedly changing the names of the meals but serving the same food nightly, we called Heiko. He arranged dinner for fifty *that evening* with two hours' notice! We ate outside at a beautiful golf course, and congratulated Heiko for having obviously ordered the absolutely perfect weather—until it got a bit chilly. But guess what! You got it! There was the amazing Heiko, armed with sweaters and sweatshirts for all who needed to warm up. We've unfortunately lost touch with Heiko, but we will never lose touch with what he taught us about passion, commitment, and leading with your heart.

The way to get stimulus into your life and yield more stimulating outcomes is to express passion in everything you do, like our friend Heiko. Let your mind surrender to your heart and the sparks that give you meaning, and surge full steam ahead with those things you feel strongly about. Passion is the emotional pump that gives energy and vitality to the creative harvesting process. Abundant yields of creative ideas cannot be obtained without the full energy and commitment of the person who comes up with the ideas—YOU! Whether you are selling mattresses or acting as chauffeur/tour guide/problem-solver extraordinaire, passion will stimulate you and help you produce significant and stimulating feats.

HE WHO LIVES IN HARMONY WITH HIMSELF LIVES IN HARMONY WITH THE UNIVERSE.

—MARCUS AURELIUS, ROMAN EMPEROR

Creative Harmony

One of the core tenets of cultural anthropology is the idea that we are selfishly motivated and our survival depends on what benefits the individual and what we do to advance our own individual genes. If this is the case, why is working together so prevalent? Very simply, sharing food production and sharing the fruitful results of a harvest is a universal human characteristic not so much because we always do things for the good of the group or society, but because it helps us share the risks of failure and increase the odds of individual success. Perhaps this explains the origin of the phrase "two heads are better than one."

The early hunting and gathering societies were meat oriented, and the acquisition of meat became a cooperative (and then later social) activity because the odds of one person being able to succeed and survive acquiring meat alone were slim. According to Matt Ridley in *The Origin of Virtues*, "meat represented luck." But even in a group, hunters only succeeded in killing anything at all about 40 percent of the time. Additionally, when the individual members of a group work together, Ridley says, "sharing spreads the risk as well as the reward." When there is more than one person to help create, more possibilities for success can be created.

Teamwork is the fuel that allows common people
to attain uncommon results.

—UNKNOWN

YOUR CREATIVE GENIUS BOARD

In the spirit of recognizing that to help fulfill our creative impulses we need to team up with others, we lead an activity with participants in our workshops around the globe that gets them imagining and planning creative genius boards.

Much like a corporate board of directors, when you need to harvest your ideas to produce dramatic results, you need the support of others. So, whether you have a specific idea now that you'd like to harvest and move forward on or you'd like to generate ideas, ask yourself, "Who might I use as my creative genius board?"

At a minimum, this board should:

- Be supportive of your endeavors
- Be willing to listen
- Offer advice, knowledge, or know-how
- Be available and accessible
- Be passionate and strategic

To a certain extent the process of creative harvesting and our chances of producing stimulating results abide by the same anthropological principles that hundreds of thousands of years ago first helped shape how we trade, exchange knowledge, and cooperate. Our ability to stimulate creative outcomes is largely dependent on our working collectively and sharing in the bounty as a way to affirm the cooperation and success of our mutually aligned ventures. In other words, while we each crave to express ourselves individually just as we desire to advance our genetic traits, many people feel the need to rely on others to help fulfill their creative impulses and aspirations. Creative harvesting is a contemporary form of foraging in which the people of any given community or organization work together to share in the process of scouting for ideas, playing with ideas, venturing toward the ideas they want to make reality, and harvesting the results of their efforts.

HELP YOUR BROTHER'S BOAT ACROSS AND **YOUR OWN** WILL REACH THE SHORE.

—Hindu proverb

If we share our stimulating, seeking, and sparking processes, the chances of generating, gathering, and assimilating ideas increases. Therefore, foraging and cooperation, as they relate to the process of harvesting sparks and ideas, represent a sort of reciprocity in which one individual's creative idea and expression work in harmony with another person's creative genius, a powerful force for advancing creative action.

Years ago we were working with an international tire company that had been struggling to be competitive and was only producing sporadic results. One of the company's tire plants—located in the southern part of the United States—had a history of infighting and low employee morale. The situation changed, however, when a new plant manager, Perry G., arrived on the scene.

Before taking this role as plant manager, Perry had earned a reputation for demonstrating an unwavering dedication to quality, teamwork, and high performance. He was also known for being able to creatively turn around situations where there seemed to be no hope. Soon after he took over and had had time to assess the situation, he addressed the organization by holding a series of roundtable discussions about morale, performance, and related issues, including mistrust and the lack of cooperation. It was clear to him that the organization was neither engaged nor very "stimulated" (his words) to produce consistent, high-quality results. He quickly identified an underlying degree of animosity and mistrust not only within management, but also between groups of individuals. From the bottom of the line to the top, there was very little trust and teamwork. "These tire-producing functions were operating in silos and consequently production goals were not possible," Perry said. One day, while attending his son's orchestra concert, he began thinking about the harmony and success of an orchestra and how it might apply to his new organizational challenge. He realized that he had an organization of talented performers but no one knew the score, and everyone was creating their own separate melody. In a memo to employees, Perry wrote the following:

I cannot undo the deeds of mistrust from times past, but I pledge to all employees my efforts to establish a new opportunity of trust and create an open and collaborative working atmosphere where we are all performing from the same song sheet so to speak and know what our roles are in creating successful harmony between functions to achieve our goals. I pledge to you that I will work feverishly to make our plant competitive again. I pledge to you that I will listen and respond to your concerns while at the same time expect that you respect my decisions that I make in the interest of the entire plant. We cannot do this alone and must work together to produce a win–win environment in which each member of this organization feels valued and has the chance to succeed as the organization succeeds.

The time to act is now, and I am therefore recommending to the organization that we implement a new business team structure that will promote shared responsibility and accountability for the entire production process. A team-based organization will help us to break down barriers, improve communications, improve trust and ultimately help us to harmonize our efforts in order to achieve our goals. In the coming months you will hear more about our plans for implementing a business team structure and training that will support our efforts to succeed in this endeavor. In the meantime, I hope that you will join me in working together and respond enthusiastically to my call for action.

While business teams and a team-based organization are not a revolutionary idea today, back in the mid-1990s when Perry was trying to turn around his plant, a business team structure was new and different. What is also important to note is that Perry's actions were the result of a spark he had while watching his son's orchestra concert. In thinking about how an orchestra plays, he recognized that while every musician may have a special role, what makes an orchestra produce effective and stimulating music is that every member must operate from the same sheet of music and hit their respective notes in harmony with one another. For Perry, building an effective tire plant depended on directing his creative energies toward the whole. As we cultivate the conditions for creative action and venture into new territories, we must remember that the process of producing stimulating outcomes of growth, change, and bringing ideas to life depends on the mutual cooperation of individuals working in harmony with one another.

SYNERGY, **THE BONUS** THAT IS ACHIEVED WHEN THINGS **WORK TOGETHER HARMONIOUSLY.**

—MARK TWAIN, AMERICAN HUMORIST AND WRITER

Celebration

Celebrations naturally revolve around the cycles of the seasons as ways to commemorate the significant times of the year, whether we count those as the time for harvesting crops, the time for marking the new year, or the time for a family reunion. Taking part in seasonal festivities suggests to other celebrants that we share similar experiences, that we are maybe a bit more alike than we thought. Celebrations can be considered just about anything that brings us together for a good time and publicly acknowledges our accomplishments. They help stimulate our passion, our spirits, and our memories. It's hard to pass up a good party, especially when we have worked hard to accomplish something of significance. But even if you have not achieved something of great importance, the experience of celebrating with another will strengthen the bonds between us as human beings. It's stimulating to be clinking a glass, slapping a high five, or shouting gleefully in response to a moment of joy or spark of energy.

SPICE ACTIVITY

Consider planning a celebration that incorporates the traditions of a culture that you are not familiar with. Do this at home with your family or at work. Ask others to pitch in by bringing food, games, and decorations that represent the culture you are celebrating.

What rituals might you create (or adopt from others) in order to celebrate your creative yield at work or at home, or better yet, both?

Organizations and communities that lack celebration are easy to detect. They have little if any creative spunk. Instead they are zombies like the ones we described in chapter 1, bumping aimlessly and heartlessly through their workdays. It seems like nothing short of an electrical charge will bring them back to life.

However, given the opportunity to freely express themselves, to cut loose and let their hair down, it's amazing the results people can stimulate. A participant in one of our workshops, Devin M., wrote the following in a letter to us:

> I'm so grateful that I now know how important it is to celebrate. Intuitively I knew it all along but never had the courage to bring it into work. After attending your workshop, it hit me—I need to celebrate with my team on a regular basis. If nothing else, I thought it would build good relationships . . . whether or not it would have concrete results, I didn't know. But I decided to trust the process and see what might happen. So, that's exactly what I did. Well, six months after instituting a "celebration committee" specifically charged with researching the types of celebrations that the team was interested in, creating opportunities for celebrating, and documenting our celebration "case stories," an amazing thing happened—our team was given an innovation reward for not only the research and practice we had done in the area of celebration, but also the results we produced because of it. Sales for my team were up and customer feedback that we received was more positive than

before. Now, the model of what my team and I created exists across the entire organization and serves as the protocol, if you will, of how to institutionalize celebration as a way of life on a regular basis. So, I'm a believer in celebration, and my motto is "celebrate often and always, for the results you produce will have stimulating outcomes!"

As you can tell from Devin's story, she's a true believer and advocate of celebration. It's obvious how celebration can help strengthen our commitment to produce and provide the necessary release to free up our capacity to create more—and the results prove it! These celebrations don't need to cost a lot or be grand and formal. In fact, what Devin found is that the more spontaneous celebrations had a greater impact on the camaraderie and performance of her team. So, what are you waiting for? Get out there and celebrate!

While most people would agree that it is important to celebrate successes, few if any appreciate the stimulating and productive impact that a celebration may have on a more somber part of our life. Disappointments, setbacks, and losses are also a part of life. Yet without some form of celebration or ritual, we may not be able to move on and soothe the pain of our losses. To produce stimulating results, creative harvesting rituals for organizations and communities need to include the celebration of both successes and failures.

There's a party goin' on right here. A celebration to last throughout the years. So bring your good times, and your laughter too. We gonna celebrate your party with you.

—Kool and the Gang, "Celebration"

Every Spark Has a Season

Virtually every culture we are familiar with has some ceremony or ritual marking the opening and closing of the harvest period. Throughout time and across all cultures you will find many wonderful ceremonies, activities, and artifacts that pay homage to our accomplishments and express hopeful expectations about our future. These rituals may include honoring ancestors, foreseeing the future, purifying our souls, sparking new growth, creating prosperity, and much more.

One of our favorite seasons is the fall. When September rolls around, we get excited about participating in the abundant amount of activities that are associated with this time of year. We attribute our excitement to our memories of starting school, buying supplies, picking new clothes, eagerly catching up with our schoolmates, witnessing the colors of the leaves changing, and taking hikes while the days were still warm and the nights cool. From pumpkins and cornstalks to hay rides and apple picking, we delight in all that the fall season has to offer. In addition to being a time to celebrate the accomplishments of our year, it is also a time to begin preparing us for the next year.

WINTER IS AN ETCHING, SPRING A WATERCOLOR, SUMMER AN OIL PAINTING, AND AUTUMN A MOSAIC OF THEM ALL.

—STANLEY HOROWITZ, AUTHOR

Being stimulated is a seasonal commitment. Our success in activating our creative genius and producing stimulating outcomes depends on how passionate and committed we are to harvesting our sparks and our ideas. Every time we have a spark and become attracted and attached to the sprout of an idea, we have a chance to produce something of value and something that is unique to us. The expressions of our creative genius may

I'M GLAD I LIVE
WHERE SEASONS
CHANGE
I LIKE MY WORLD
TO REARRANGE.

—UNKNOWN

come in myriad forms in our work and our personal lives. One year may see us produce a revolutionary new product or finally realize our dream home, or develop a new set of relationships that brings us an abundant amount of pleasure and enjoyment. No matter what form our creative genius takes, the quality and texture of that expression will vary from year to year like the seasons of our lives.

To yield promising and stimulating outcomes, we have identified three important "seasonal" rituals that will increase the likelihood of boosting our creative output. The first joins our passion and desires to express ourselves to the world; the second pertains to how we come together and harmonize aligned creative expressions and output; and the third brings us together to celebrate and create structures (rituals) of celebration in order to affirm our interdependence and perpetuate stimulating outcomes.

Every season comes with the opportunity to produce stimulating outcomes that enable you to express your passion and enjoy the success you achieve in cooperation with others. Sometimes our spark moments will ignite a bonfire of possibilities, while other times they flicker for only a moment. Either way, the key is that when you have those spark moments, take the time to consider the possibilities, and if one spark or another adheres and appeals to you, then blaze a trail and harvest to your heart's content!

TIPS FOR HARVESTING

- Take one of your sparks and translate it into a tangible idea: Play with it, sketch it out, talk with someone else about it, and "massage" the spark until a clear picture of what you have cultivated comes into your mind.
- Come up with many ideas by building on the initial idea—the crazier your ideas, the better. It will lead you where you need to go.
- Begin a harvesting journal—capture your thoughts, sparks, and ideas and write or sketch them in the journal. Keep it close by so that it's available when you feel stimulated!

- Borrow rituals from other countries as a way to stimulate more of your own to keep your passion and creative energy alive!
- Be passionate (have we said this enough?) about what you want and go after it.
- Recruit members of your creative board today! Even just one supportive board member could be the difference between harvested ideas and those that are never given a chance.
- Make it a habit to celebrate successes and failures at home and at work; think of all the ways you might be able to add more "celebration" into your life. Do it tomorrow.
- Think about what "celebration" means to you and to others at home or at work. Why are celebrations important? What would you like your celebrations to communicate to others?
- List all the ways you could celebrate—impromptu, or planned formal gatherings, or the first Friday of the month. Remember how the characters in "Alice in Wonderland" celebrated "un-birthdays." Why have a birthday celebration only once a year? It's more fun to have celebrations every day!
- Remember that mutual cooperation is the best way to reap the rewards of the seeds you have sown—so be sure to gather others and truly act as a team to get things done!
- Plant a flower or grow a garden—watch how the seeds come to life as they are intended to; use this as a metaphor for how you will take your sparks of ideas and make them real!

CHAPTER 8

Keeping in Swing: Sustaining Your Creative Genius

On the rare occasion when we find ourselves not knowing quite what to do with some extra time, we go digging through our library of books, games, and movies hoping to find much-needed relaxation to wash the dust of everyday life from our minds and souls. Watching movies has always been a fun pastime for us as a way to get out of our own "stuff," escape a bit from reality, and just hang out. Movies, coupled with a fresh bowl of popcorn we cook the old-fashioned way (on the stove, in a kettle), can be the perfect combination for resting muscles weary from trying to balance busy work and personal schedules. We're sure you can relate to how responsibility and commitments keep things busy!

Movies can also be a great source of stimulus. One of our personal favorites is *Bagger Vance,* starring Matt Damon, Will Smith, and Charlize Theron. It's a very entertaining and heartwarming film about a young man (Damon) who, after returning from WWI, struggles with the scars of his wartime experiences and slips into exile under the dulling effects of alcohol. Previously a gifted golfer, Junuh, the young man, now has no interest in pursing the dreams of his past. Then opportunity knocks and the field of possibilities emerges for him. At first he resists the chance to reengage with his past success. However, he eventually agrees, and enters a historic tournament by way of divine intervention, delivered by his caddy, Bagger Vance (Smith). Junuh returns to the game he so loved and excelled in and develops a relationship not only with his caddy, but also with a lover lost in the space of time and transition. He slowly realizes he has "lost his grip and swing on life." He sees the tournament as a chance to catch one last moment of glory.

Movies

What are some of your favorite movies? How about some from your child-hood? Plan a day or evening and rent one of these old movies. Enjoy the freedom it gives your mind to drift into an imaginary story.

Go online and search for the movies your favorite actor has been in and rent one that you've never seen. Especially fun are those that came out before some of our favorite stars were famous.

Now you don't have to be a golf aficionado to appreciate the moral of the story and how anyone may lose his or her swing and, as a result, feel unstimulated about life. (Remember David from Dublin?) The trick is, as the movie suggests, to find your swing—your "authentic swing" that is in harmony with who you are and what you can be in relationship to your world. Finding your authentic swing means finding a natural rhythm in which to express yourself, or as we have been saying throughout this book—our creative genius. Your swing is the outward manifestation of your creative genius. The more you are able to develop your "creative swing," the more you are exercising your creative genius.

ARE YOU GENUINE?
OR JUST AN ACTOR?
A REPRESENTATIVE?
OR WHAT IT IS THAT IS REPRESENTED?
IN THE END, YOU MIGHT MERELY BE
SOMEONE MIMICKING
AN ACTOR...

—FRIEDRICH NIETZSCHE,
GERMAN PHILOSOPHER

Finding Your Creative Swing

From the moment we are born into this world we are free to experience and imagine the world as we want. Our creative genius is infinitely pliable, forever stretching, bending, and molding in response to the continuous forms of stimulus. We first receive this stimulus through our parents, and then through a world full of objects, sounds, colors, tastes, smells, and circumstances. Every individual is born into this world with a creative, authentic genius that swings like no other. How we walk, talk, laugh, listen, run, play, work, and relate is unique. At the core of our creative genius and our swing, there is a world rich with stimuli, possibilities, adventures, sparks, ideas, and transformations. How we experience them, make sense of them, and transform them into a reflection of our creative genius is deeply individual. We have an amazing capacity to be stimulated and stimulate endless possibilities through our own creative swing with life. Nothing seems too difficult nor out of bounds when we are in full swing, exercising our creative genius and sparking possibilities.

DOING WHAT YOU LOVE
IS THE CORNERSTONE OF
HAVING ABUNDANCE
IN YOUR LIFE.

—WAYNE DYER, AUTHOR, SPEAKER

DID YOU KNOW?

Did you know that Tiger Woods, whose golf swing is the most powerful and accurate in professional golf today, putted against Bob Hope on the "Mike Douglas Show" at age two, shot forty-eight for nine holes at age three, and was featured in *Golf Digest* at age five?

However, as time progresses, we mature, learn certain rules, and become conditioned in response to boundaries imposed by our parents, schools, friends, and workplaces. Over time we start to adjust—sometimes positively, sometimes negatively—our creative swing for life. When we are most in touch with our creative swing is when we feel that wonderful euphoric sensation associated with being stimulated. These are times when we feel most alive and excited because we are acting and responding in ways that are authentically aligned with our creative selves—our creative genius.

On the flip side, life happens, and like the character in *Bagger Vance*, we lose our grip, lose our confidence, feel overwhelmed, and in the extreme cases, even retreat from life with artificial forms of stimulus. There is, however, hope. If you ever get a chance to rent *Bagger Vance*, you will understand that no matter how challenging our life circumstances may be, we have a choice to maintain our creative genius or revive it when it has gone dormant or is seemingly in exile.

The key to maintaining and sustaining your creative genius is through a conscious choice of seeking, absorbing, and relating to the "field of stimulus" that puts us in harmony with who we are and what we wish to become.

We need to find the courage to say no to the things and people that are not serving us if we want to rediscover ourselves and live our lives with authenticity.

—Barbara de Angelis, American speaker, author, and television personality

Although it is natural for us to create and maintain our authentic creative genius, like the game of golf, it takes practice. Practice helps us to establish the highly specific routines and rituals that are necessary for sparking our creative genius. In other words, if we don't make the time, spend the time, and work toward disciplining ourselves in being stimulated, the odds are that our creative selves will atrophy and diminish. Just as with any good fitness program or diet, the key is to adhere to a set of habits that allows you to come into full possession of your creative genius. "We are what we repeatedly do," said Aristotle. "Excellence, then, is not an act, but a habit."

Habits to Maintain Your Creative Swing

Throughout this book we have tried to provide you with descriptions, stories, reflections, and other various and hopefully stimulating forms of application to help inspire you to develop your creative swing and make it relevant for you. Each of the habits we discussed—scouting, cultivating, playing, venturing, and harvesting—has certain underlying principles that are relevant to each of us, yet at the same time, may be expressed differently

What is a habit? It's a repeated, often
unconscious pattern of behavior that is
acquired through frequent repetition.

from one person to the next. Your creative swing is different from the next person's. That's not only okay, it is also key to sustaining your own unique creative genius. Your swing, or how you express yourself creatively, is the core of your creative genius, and stimulus is the catalyst that helps spark novel and exciting paths. This allows you to tap into and experience that which you were born to create. The important thing is to understand and internalize that all the habits are interconnected and working together to help you in your creative journey. Sparking your creative genius is based on how well you practice each habit to find stimulus, play with stimulus, nurture the sparks into ideas, take risks based on your ideas, and then harvest ideas into productive and flowing "swings" resulting in innovations or creative solutions that help you (and others) personally and professionally. Let's take another look at these habits and turn our attention to key principles for sustaining, rediscovering, and fine-tuning your creative genius swing.

We are what we repeatedly do. Excellence, then,
is not an act, but a habit.

—ARISTOTLE, GREEK PHILOSOPHER

Creative Genius Is About Discovery

In chapter 3, "Eyes Wide Open," we talked about the fact that we have so many different opportunities to enrich our lives that the first step to achieving success and experiencing flow with the habit of scouting is just walking out the door and being open to the possibilities. An amazing field awaits us each and every day, so what you are waiting for?

Scouting is a voyage of discovery: discovery of other people, the world, and most importantly, yourself. The voyage within is the most important one of all. Finding out more about what motivates you creatively and how you want to express that will help you choose experiences, situations, and relationships that will be the most stimulating for you. When you begin to play your creative game, you start to feel in flow, and things seem to occur naturally and effortlessly. Scouting is a perfect way to "enliven" your creative swing.

Marco Polo, perhaps the most famous Western traveler, was the personification of a scout. He was a determined traveler, writer, observer, and storyteller. For over twenty-five years he traveled Asia, and he became a trusted advisor to China's Kublai Khan before returning to Venice. His life story is the ultimate travelogue for stimulus! So, go out and develop your own road memoir of creative observation and discovery.

—Rainer Maria Rilke,
Austro-German lyric poet, novelist

Creative Genius Is About Conditioning

Conditioning, or practicing and establishing the right conditions for success, is fundamental to achieving creative expression, just as it is with every great performance. If conditions are not ripe, your performance and state of mind will suffer. The more you can embrace and cultivate your environment and develop the appropriate routines for staying creatively fit, the more likely it is that you will produce stimulating results—and, as a result, feel stimulated. Spontaneity and creative action are made possible when we intentionally leverage our functional and aesthetic environment to achieve "optimal performance and experience." This is our creative swing, the outward manifestation of your creative genius. When the conditions of the playing field favor us, we increase the likelihood of our success. So keep in mind that it is important to condition yourself to be ready to respond to the ebb and flow of life, which at times may seem capricious and unfair. However they appear, however, our life experiences offer many opportunities for us to use our creative genius.

Creative Genius Is About Imagination

If you are ever lacking creative ideas or inspiration, just hang out with a group of young children and groove to their tempo as best as you can, and we guarantee that you will find the play in your creative swing again. So long as we are willing to partake in the game of life and use our imagination, we have a good chance of succeeding, accomplishing some extraordinary things, and having some wonderful experiences. Indulge yourself and just "push play" to turn up the volume for expressing yourself, going with the flow, or inventing something new. Let your imagination be your guide.

IMAGINATION WILL OFTEN CARRY US TO WORLDS THAT NEVER WERE. BUT WITHOUT IT, WE GO NOWHERE.

—CARL SAGAN, AMERICAN ASTRONOMER AND ASTROPHYSICIST

Creative Genius Is About Courage

As soon as you begin to hear yourself saying words like *should, could, would have, could have,* you know you are second-guessing yourself. Blaise Pascal bet that it is "better to believe in God than not," based on the premise that the "expected value" of believing is always greater than the expected value of not believing. Our interpretation: if you believe in your genius and venture forth with that belief, the probability of success and value that you receive will be greater than if you don't believe in it.

After a dramatic and triumphant win in the Eastern NBA Conference Finals in 2007, all eyes were on this young upstart Cleveland Cavaliers team going up against the Goliath and perennial winner, the San Antonio Spurs. Whether you read the articles in the paper, listened to the sports talk shows, or talked to friends, everyone expected that San Antonio would win. And guess what, they did. The opposite seemed true for the Cavaliers. No one expected them to win—not the sports prognosticators, nor the many of the citizens of Cleveland who tend to attribute every loss or disappointment to some curse, not the broadcasters, not even some of the players. Perhaps if the team and collective community of supporters had diverted all of their creative and positive energies toward believing, the outcome might have been different for them.

If you believe in your creative capabilities and expressions, you will attract sparks. The more sparks you attract, the more your energy and confidence will increase and propel you toward your genius. So what are you waiting for? Go ahead, jump into your court of creative possibilities!

MUSIC IS YOUR OWN EXPERIENCE, YOUR THOUGHTS, YOUR WISDOM. IF YOU DON'T LIVE IT, IT WON'T COME OUT YOUR HORN.

—CHARLIE PARKER, AMERICAN JAZZ SAXOPHONIST
AND COMPOSER

PRACTICE MAKES PERFECT, AS LONG AS YOU CATCH SOME GOOD ZZZS

A study done by Harvard Medical School suggests that practice makes perfect, as long as you get a good night's sleep. According to Matter Walker, senior author of the paper describing the research, "Motor skill learning is maximized when we get a full night's sleep. You could say that modern life's erosion of sleep time is seriously shortchanging your brain of valuable learning potential." The research demonstrates that, after a certain amount of time, more practice may not be what's needed, but instead perhaps more sleep!

To stay creatively fit and access your genius, practice and power sleep make perfect!

Creative Genius Is About Richness and Reach

Because we are all unique, we have an abundant number of ways to express ourselves and produce rich results as long as we stay true to ourselves. The secret of harvesting stimulating outcomes is to be yourself. As soon as you sense you are losing your swing or have to contort to unnatural boundaries and conditions imposed upon you by others, it is time to play on another course. As the old saying goes, life is short, so don't waste your time cultivating a creative persona and ethic that is not authentically you. Your rich creative expression is waiting to be mined in your individual creative genius.

At the same time, you will want to pursue your own creative path while working in harmony with others who are finding ways to express themselves. Although we are unique, we also have many things in common, and when we work together, we take advantage of the reach we can obtain through collective creative power. To harvest your creative genius, help others tend their own creative ground. We are people of the hearth, communal creatures, and we experience great joy and accomplishment when we work together and create space for mutually aligned creative expression. This is how organizations and communities can innovate.

IF YOU CALL FORTH
WHAT IS IN YOU,
IT WILL SAVE YOU.
IF YOU DO NOT CALL FORTH WHAT IS IN YOU,
IT WILL DESTROY YOU.

—St. Thomas Aquinas, Italian
PRIEST, PROFESSOR, AND PHILOSOPHER

Sustaining Your Creative Genius

To grow and maintain our creative genius and be in full, stimulated swing, we must practice the five habits—scouting, cultivating, playing, venturing, and harvesting. In addition to these habits, we recommend keeping in mind the following set of sustaining principles that will help you live a creative life.

The first principle is to *have a clear sense of your destination and creative genius, your "swing potential."* Not everyone is cut out to be Picasso, but that should not stop us from painting or expressing ourselves in artistic ways. The key here is to think hard, take time, and reflect upon those moments, circumstances, places, people, events, objects, and happenings that sparked you most, when you felt yourself at your most creative. Having an honest and accurate perception of your creative genius is important to orienting yourself to your life.

There is an old story about a mischievous young boy who played a trick on an eagle by placing one of the eagle's eggs in the nest of a chicken. The boy forgot about his trick, and eventually the eagle hatched under the protection of one of the mother hens. Unaware of his true creative potential, the eagle lived his life as a chicken. He developed the same habits as the other chickens and ate the same food. Then one day he saw an eagle flying above him, and suddenly he yearned to fly like the eagle. The other chickens said, "Don't be silly, you are just a chicken." He believed the chickens and didn't even attempt to fly. Sadly, the fate of the eagle describes the destiny of many people who fail to assess themselves and their true creative potential. Life may play tricks on us from time to time, but the real challenge is to recognize that although we might be temporarily "cooped up," we can and must figure out how to soar with our authentic creative self.

So, in order to have a clear sense of your creative genius, start with a vision—draw it out, write it out in the form of goals, collage it, mind-map it, get down on paper what it is you want and how you want to soar. Then, determine where you are now. Make an assessment of your creative goals and your strengths and determine the steps you can take *today* to begin to realize them. Finally, once you've got all this data to look at, let it speak to you. That which you have drawn, sketched, doodled, and written will give you a not-so-subtle glimpse (or a big smack in the face!) of how you want to express yourself in this world. What is it telling you? Don't be afraid to hear what your creation has to say.

Our deepest fear is not that we are inadequate. Our deepest fear is that we are powerful beyond measure. It is our light, not our darkness that frightens us most. We ask ourselves, "Who am I to be brilliant, gorgeous, talented, and famous?" Actually, who are you not to be? Your playing small does not serve the world. There is nothing enlightened about shrinking so that people won't feel insecure around you. When we let our light shine we unconsciously give other people permission to do the same.

—MARYANN WILLIAMSON, AUTHOR

The second principle is to *get out and get stimulated!* Just as we emphasized with the habits of scouting, playing, and venturing, it is really important to just get yourself started with the process of attracting and advancing stimulus to help you explore your creative side and help others do the same. When it comes to being stimulated, we are not unbiased. We are partisans. Spark moments are in the universe waiting for us to capture them, shape them, and apply them to our everyday lives so that we can live more freely, generate new possibilities, and feel more alive. The powerful presence of stimulus helps us engage more deeply with others and with our world, and as a result we feel abundance and joy. As MaryAnn Williamson says, our "playing small does not serve the world." So the question for each of us is, How might I play big?

THE AUTHENTIC!
SHADOWS OF IT SWEEP PAST IN DREAMS,
ONE COULD SAY IMPRECISELY,
EVOKING THE ALMOST-SILENT
RIPPING APART OF GIANT
SHEETS OF CELLOPHANE.

—DENISE LEVERTOV, AMERICAN POET

The third principle is to *stretch yourself.* Sometimes we need to stretch ourselves and take ourselves out of our comfort zones to try new things and explore new terrains. Oliver Wendell Holmes once said, "A man's mind stretched to a new idea never goes back to its original dimensions." The beauty of being stimulated by engaging in more experiences and experimenting with different ideas and concepts is that your mind will, in fact, stretch. And that stretching will unleash your creative genius to do what it is that you are passionate about and attract more of it into your life.

Expert golfers become "expert" not by playing on the same course but by developing their skill on different courses. Therefore, as you consider your potential and your desired expectation for tapping into that supple creative side of yours, consider trying new things in order to maximize your game for creating.

The fourth principle is to *track your successes.* Just about any self-help or people development–related book or seminar will tell you the importance of self-reflection and examination. It is essential to sustaining your creative genius to journal your activity so that you see progress and make adjustments along your creative journey as needed. We are constantly evolving and new opportunities are always emerging, so it is important to document the paths you take to build up the necessary momentum and keep you on your creative path.

And finally, the last principle is to *be faithful to your creative genius.* The nature of life at times seems to tip us out of balance, stress us out, and overwhelm us to the point we stray from our true creative selves. Or unfortunate circumstances prevail and our creative desires and expressions are called into question—either the people or the setting around us taint the canvas upon which we wish to make our mark. When this happens, our creative genius is at its most vulnerable. Depending on the magnitude of the change and the pressure of the force that challenges us, we may abandon our creative genius in exchange for a safer and more conservative path.

As seasoned travelers through both personal and professional change, we understand how important it is to rely upon our creative genius. In good times and in bad, the choices we make every day will keep us either faithful or unfaithful to the path that is ours to journey. When you put these habits in place and find your "swing," you will feel your creative genius within every cell of your being. You'll attract spark moments and feel passion, excitement, invigoration, motivation, and energy. You'll know that possibilities abound through your imagination. You'll be excited, refreshed, and alive—in essence, you will be stimulated!

FRESHNESS
SPARK MOMENTS
PASSION
INVIGORATION